TOUCHING GROUND

TOUCHING GROUND

Devotion and Demons
along the Path to Enlightenment

TIM TESTU

Edited by Emma Varvaloucas

Introduction by Jeanette Testu

Foreword by Jaimal Yogis

Wisdom Publications
199 Elm Street
Somerville, MA 02144 USA
wisdompubs.org

Library of Congress Cataloging-in-Publication Data
Names: Heng Ju, Bhikshu, 1944–1998, author. | Container of (work): Heng Ju, Bhikshu, 1944–1998. Three steps, one bow.
Title: Touching ground : devotion and demons along the path to enlightenment / Tim Testu; edited by Emma Varvaloucas; introduction by Jeanette Testu.
Description: Somerville, MA : Wisdom Publications, 2018. |
Identifiers: LCCN 2017052938 (print) | LCCN 2018002935 (ebook) | ISBN 9781614293446 (ebook) | ISBN 9781614293330 (pbk.: alk. paper)
Subjects: LCSH: Heng Ju, Bhikshu, 1944–1998. | Zen Buddhists—United States—Biography. | Buddhist monks—United States—Biography.
Classification: LCC BQ962.E64 (ebook) | LCC BQ962.E64 A3 2018 (print) | DDC 294.3/92092 [B] —dc23
LC record available at https://lccn.loc.gov/2017052938

ISBN 978-1-61429-333-0   ebook ISBN 978-1-61429-344-6

22 21 20 19 18   5 4 3 2 1

Cover design by Philip Pascuzzo. Interior design by Tony Lulek. Set in ITC Galliard Pro 10/16.2.

Excerpted text from *Three Steps, One Bow,* © 1977 Sino-American Buddhist Association (first edition) ISBN 978-1-60103-074-0 (paperback)
Reprinted with permission by Buddhist Text Translation Society
4951 Bodhi Way, Ukiah, CA 95482, www.buddhisttexts.org
For a complete copy, see the latest edition in ebook *Three Steps, One Bow: American Buddhist Monks' 1,100-Mile Journey for World Peace,* © 2014 Buddhist Text Translation Society, ISBN 978-1-60103-074-0 (ebook)

Wisdom Publications' books are printed on acid-free paper and meet the guidelines for permanence and durability of the Production Guidelines for Book Longevity of the Council on Library Resources.

♻This book was produced with environmental mindfulness. For more information, please visit wisdompubs.org/wisdom-environment.

Printed in the United States of America.

CONTENTS

FOREWORD

"Good medicine is bitter to the taste."

So goes a Chinese proverb, one that Dharma Master Hsuan Hua was fond of quoting. I remember hearing it for the first time at the monastery Master Hua founded: the City of Ten Thousand Buddhas in Ukiah, California.

"The City," as its frequenters and residents often call it for short, is not nearly as well-known in Western Buddhist circles as, say, Tassajara or Spirit Rock. But it should be. It might be the largest Buddhist monastery in the United States, as well as one of the most celebrated in Taiwan and China.

My friend Gene and I had both just started to explore Eastern contemplative practices when we met at a month-long youth yoga retreat in Grass Valley. We were nineteen years old. We had to sweep and garden to earn free room and board at the ashram, but other than having to do a little shoveling, everything was easy. There were lots of teachers suggesting that we "just relax, breathe, and enjoy life's beauty." So we did. The ashram was full of beautiful, healthy people. We all ate piles of yummy vegetarian food, sang songs around the bonfire, stretched for hours every morning, swam in the crystalline Yuba River, and talked about God as love. It was a happy summer.

But in the midst of this summer of love, another yogi on the retreat had rattled our peace. His name was Daniel. He had a full brown beard and cutting green eyes. Dan had just come from living at the City for a month. And when he spoke of Master Hua or the monastery, he whispered, as if he'd stumbled upon a mythical land.

"It's more Chinese than China," Daniel told us as we all ate vegetarian chili and salad in the middle of one of the ashram's many flowering meadows. "They practice Chan to the letter, just like it was done during the Tang Dynasty. The monks and nuns have vows to never lie down. They meditate, I kid you not, *all night long*."

"What's *Chan*?" I asked.

Daniel laughed. "It's Zen. Before it went soft."

Daniel was only joking. Japanese Zen is plenty hardcore. But he was trying to explain to us rookies that there were other approaches to spirituality than singing around a campfire—approaches that he said could put our yoga practice into hyperdrive.

Having only recently started a modest meditation practice—I was struggling to make twenty minutes a day—the idea of sitting in lotus all night long gave me chills. And as if that weren't enough, Daniel said the City had been an insane asylum before Master Hua converted it to a monastery. The monks and nuns slept in the former cells of the patients: three-foot-thick walls, the works. Some of the monks had gone on pilgrimages around the United States just like they used to do fifteen hundred years ago in China. "It's called 'three steps, one bow,'" Daniel said. "They take three steps and then do a full prostration—knees, hands, and forehead on the ground. And they walk like that down highways and over mountains with bloody knees and hands, trying to transcend every last attachment to comfort—anything that could obstruct full buddhahood." He said that most Western spiritual centers were trying to soften the true Dharma so they didn't turn people off. If we wanted the real thing—no filter—we should check out the City's summer Chan session, where the monks sat fourteen hours each day.

As we sucked down mango smoothies, Gene and I joked that the City sounded like torture. Why would we ever leave California yoga heaven for Chinese pain? But Daniel kept telling us stories about the City—how the monks positively glowed; how many of them took on ascetic practices but some didn't, because it was their choice. And how ascetic or not, they were all jovial, warm, even funny. Gene and I weren't sure if we were terrified or envious of Dan's experience, but we couldn't stop asking questions. And by the time we'd scraped the last bites of sprouts and nuts from our bowls, we knew that we were going to go on our own pilgrimage to the City of Ten Thousand Buddhas. Maybe we wouldn't do "three steps, one bow," but walking from my mom's house in Sacramento seemed like the least we could do to earn our stripes for our first real-deal Chan session.

We wanted some bitter medicine.

It was late July when Gene and I started our walk. By 8:00 a.m., the temperature had already reached the high 90s. By the time we arrived in Davis later that afternoon—where we'd sleep in a ditch behind a car dealership—it was about 115 degrees.

Gene and I were embarking on a journey of two hundred miles through the sinuous back roads of wine country. We hoped to finish it in a week in order to arrive in time for the City's summer meditation session. That meant about thirty miles a day of walking—more than either of us had ever attempted.

When Gene and I finally passed through the Tang Dynasty–style gates of the City later that summer, our feet were covered in blisters, our noses were peeling from sunburn, and our backs ached with pain. To prepare ourselves for the extremes we knew we'd be enduring, we slept on the ground along the way and ate mostly berries and other things we could forage from the side of the road. It seems crazy to me now that we wanted to do any of this, but without ever hearing him speak or reading one of his books, the Master Hua approach had gotten under our skin.

Walking around the City felt like being in another time. Peacocks roamed wild under massive pagodas and grand bronze Buddha statues. Bald-headed monks and nuns with the traditional incense burns branded on the tops of their skulls scurried about reciting the names of buddhas and prostrating just about everywhere there was a buddha statue (and there literally are ten thousand). Daniel met us there and he informed one of the senior laymen about our pilgrimage. The layman was so thrilled that he invited Gene and me to speak to the sangha that very evening about why we had attempted something so "wonderful and sincere" like suffering in the heat for a week. We felt—at first—like our hard work was paying dividends.

Of course, we would only be able to meet the great Dharma master himself in dreams, in which he told us to work harder; this was 1998, and the Master had died in 1995. (Though we were invited to view Master Hua's crystallized bones: the parts of him that didn't burn during cremation and that were believed to maintain some of the master's power.) But everything Daniel had said about the City turned out to be true. That first Chan retreat felt like trying to run an ultramarathon after training with a few laps around the block. We spent weeks suffering through brutal knee pain, meditating and listening to Master Hua's recorded lectures about Chan retreats in old China—I recall distinctly one about monks who died during Chan retreats and how they were simply thrown under the Chan bench until the retreat was over. Unlike at most meditation centers, where a teacher might say, "Well, go easy on yourself—try lying down," the teachers at the City would say, "Pain! That's great. Keeps the mind present. Use it as your meditation topic."

Where in the hell were we?

During that first retreat, I almost left the City many times. It often felt like the place really was an insane asylum. But after a few weeks, Gene and I noticed something. Sure, we might not be meditating all night long. But sitting for, say, a couple of hours suddenly wasn't difficult. In fact, it was quite peaceful. Pain was relative. And as the body became accustomed to this seemingly rigid form, we could finally start to watch the mind's more subtle movements. This "go-hard-or-go-home" Buddhism had trained us to do something in a month that, at the start of this summer, we hadn't thought we'd ever be able to do. Discipline *worked*. Hard work *worked*. And the result was more freedom.

Dan had been right about something else too. The monks at the City of Ten Thousand Buddhas were different than any other human beings we'd ever met. Austere as they could seem, if you spoke to them, they were warm, intelligent—and often hilarious. Inspired by these people who seemed like spiritual superheroes, when the retreat ended, I went to live at one of the City's branch monasteries in Berkeley to learn from Heng Sure, one of Master Hua's oldest disciples. For a while I even thought about ordaining.

Since my time at the City of Ten Thousand Buddhas, I've tried lots of different meditation approaches—from gentle to devotional to hard-as-nails—and in my experience, they are all helpful. You find what suits your nature at different times of life. But whenever I'm enduring anything difficult, I hear Master Hua's voice in my ear: "Good medicine is bitter to the taste." And I know—from experience—that it's true.

It's often said that there are eighty-eight thousand Dharma doors and that the path to enlightenment is a razor's edge. Hard practice can be helpful, but picking up your macho vajra sword to try to be some spiritual hero can easily become another ego trip. You can find yourself quite a bit worse off than before you ever started.

It seems Master Hua was an expert at bringing students to their limit, then reeling them back before they went too far. But even with a teacher as skilled as Master Hua, the mind is complicated. When do we push harder? And when do we give our egos a break?

I don't think I have ever read a story that explains the subtlety of this challenge with more honesty, humor, and humanity than Tim Testu's *Touching Ground*. From his battles with alcohol and the law to his struggles with relationships and faith, Tim seems to be telling us about the universal challenge of being alive. He was a gifted storyteller with a rare vulnerability—a quality that I imagine came from his sincere practice. In addition, by recording his stories of the City of Ten Thousand Buddhas for a wide audience, Tim has given the Buddhist community a rare gift.

Whether you meditate or not, this book is a great epic—one that ultimately illustrates a profound truth: our mistakes are our teachers.

Jaimal Yogis
San Francisco, California

INTRODUCTION

I knew my dad had been writing a lot. He would wake up early every morning, make a hot breakfast, walk the dog, meditate for an hour, write for an hour. Then he would wake me up and report his activities, suggesting that I too should get up and do something vigorous, worthy, contemplative. He would also have a hot breakfast waiting for me.

After he died in 1998, while I was cleaning out his study I found a life insurance policy I never knew he had taken out hidden in his desk drawer. Lying next to it was a floppy disk. Written in big block letters across the disk, inked in Sharpie marker, were the words: "JETTI PLEASE PUBLISH OR GIVE TO THE BUDDHISTS. THIS IS MY LAST AND FINAL WISH." The disk contained an account of his entire life, spanning almost two hundred pages, documenting everything from his time as a submariner in the United States Navy to his "hippie days" on an anarchist commune.

I was grateful to have a record of his adventures. I knew that his friends and the rest of the family would be interested in reading it, too. But I was surprised and horrified to see that he expected me to publish the damn thing. (Of all the moral teachings my father learned in his study of Chinese Buddhism, I think filial piety was his favorite.)

I was eighteen years old, heartbroken over his death, and didn't exactly have a lot of contacts in the publishing world. With a mixed feeling of dread and duty, I moved the disk, his notebooks, and the computer itself dozens of times with me, from student housing in Arizona to a houseboat in Seattle; from Bellingham, Edmonds, Poulsbo, and Port Townsend, and then back to Seattle again, always keeping it in the small secret drawer of the dresser he had built me.

Somewhere along the way, the disk got lost. I was relieved of the burden—but sad that I had let him down. I knew his was an unfair request to make from the grave, something I would never impose on my own child. Still, I wanted to make him happy. Also, I was pretty sure his ghost would know I had failed at my task and would come to scold me in my dreams. With the disk left unpublished, our karma was left unresolved. My dad believed in reincarnation. What if he came back as my cat or—my God—my child? He had such a powerful presence. Anything was possible.

I had been raised in the Chan (Chinese Zen) tradition, but as time went by I fell away from the Buddhist community, stopped honoring the five precepts, got a job, got married, had a baby. Then a few years ago I was invited to the Buddha's birthday celebration at a monastery in Washington where I knew a lot of my dad's old Dharma friends would be. Sure enough, I saw Dharma Master Heng Lai, the abbot of Snow Mountain Monastery, who had known him in the seventies. He said he had a copy of my dad's manuscript in a zip file and could email it to me if I wanted. He sent it to me the next day. It was time to take action on my father's last and final wish.

My dad was an American monk named Heng Ju (Tim Testu), a disciple of Venerable Master Hsuan Hua, whom he referred to simply as "the master." Hsuan Hua had come from Hong Kong to California in 1962, after having previously directed followers to establish the Dharma Realm Buddhist Association, from which many affiliated monasteries and centers would spring, including the City of Ten Thousand Buddhas, one of the first Chan temples in the United States and one of the largest Buddhist compounds in the Western Hemisphere, where my dad lived on and off throughout his life. The monastery is known for its insistence on strict adherence to the traditional monastic code; the keeping of the five precepts was strongly encouraged, and participating in ascetic practices like eating one meal a day and sleeping while sitting up were commended. In 1973, my dad and another monk, Heng Yo, began a ten-month bowing pilgrimage for world peace through California, Oregon, and Washington, traveling over a thousand miles on foot. It was the first "three steps, one bow" pilgrimage in the history of American Buddhism.

Dad finished his autobiography shortly before he died. It gives the perspective of an older (and maybe wiser) man with a complicated life: two ex-wives, a teenage daughter, alcoholism, and a cancer diagnosis.

Before seeing Heng Lai, I never knew why Dad had left the monastery. I did know how fervently he'd loved his life as a monk and how he respected and adored his teacher. The family mythology was that he had sneaked out in the middle of the night, crawling on the dried-up riverbed instead of walking out through the main gate. I thought this was a little dramatic, but then, all of his stories about the monastery were dramatic.

The reason he left had something to do with shame. He had gone out drinking as a monk, breaking a basic precept. This was after being ordained for almost a decade, after completing his bowing pilgrimage, after hundreds of newspaper articles had been written about the trip and he had written his own book about it, and after touring Asia with the master, giving Dharma talks to the sangha. The fall from grace was too difficult for him to face.

I know about shame.

Dad had leukemia for six years before he died, and I did not understand how ill he was because the man never, ever complained. We lived *way* out in the country on the Olympic Peninsula, on a waterfront property with an assortment of tents, trailers, and dogs, and garden hoses and electric cords draped from trees. We had an outhouse, an outdoor kitchen, and an outdoor bathtub. This may sound like hippie Zen paradise—unless you are a twelve-year-old with menstrual cramps, a bad haircut, a bad attitude, and no friends for forty miles. To me, his cancer treatments meant a field trip to Seattle—hospital french fries, veggie burgers, going for Chinese just the two of us.

Dad used every available minute we had together to "transmit the Dharma" to me, lecturing on everything from vegetarianism and respectable conduct to small-engine repair, how to vote (Democratic), how to hold your breath underwater, how to drive a stick shift, how to chop vegetables (according to their nature), how to identify good music (clean, crisp, and stinkin' with the groove), how to identify poisonous mushrooms, and most important, how to avoid ego and suffering through cultivating the Way. But like most kids, I was full of desires. I wanted to be pretty, thin, popular. I wanted to curl my hair, wear cute outfits, and laugh with my friends. I wanted a living room with a couch and a big TV instead of a meditation hall. And I certainly did *not* want my dad dropping me off at school dances on the back of his gold BMW motorcycle. His answer to me asking for these things was usually some version of "Do not give rise to a single thought." I was embarrassed by my dad's devotion to Buddhism, tired of the constant smell of incense.

At the end of his life, Dad asked me to come home from college to take care of him, and I did. But we had a fight over my frivolous spending. He asked me to pitch in on the mortgage, and I had spent all my money on vanilla lattes and shoes. Rather than admit I was wrong, I moved out. The night he went to the hospital for the last time, we were supposed to have met, to go out to dinner and make up.

As an adult, I can see the profound grace in a strict routine, the joy in hard work, and the relief of not being driven by emotions. I see a lot of wisdom now in the way my dad conducted his life, though I rejected it for a long time. I wish I had known that we wouldn't have many years together in this life and that my teenage rebellion was a luxury I did not have time for. (Which for me was becoming a born-again Christian, because how else was I supposed to piss off a recovering alcoholic Buddhist monk?)

What I wish more than anything is that my dad could have lived to enjoy his grandson. I think they would have really dug watching Miyazaki films and *My Name Is Earl* and going to comic conventions together. I'd love to argue about politics and cook farmer's market veggies while we listen to NPR. Or set him up with my gorgeous fifty-seven-year-old salsa-dancing friend (though I suspect he would have become a monastic again if he had lived). I'd love to listen to his stories and ask more questions, like how to beat the howling loneliness when I wake up at night or how to let go of the thirst for happiness. And I'd love to thank him for his caring attentiveness to me. And for writing the story of his heart.

Thank you to the fabulous Emma Varvaloucas for setting this book in motion by selecting the last chapter of the then-unpublished manuscript to be published in the Fall 2014 issue of *Tricycle: The Buddhist Review* and for beautifully editing this complete manuscript. Her talent is as enormous as her heart. And thank you to Wisdom Publications for granting my father's wish and releasing me from my karmic debt.

This book is a dream come true for two people. This book is a life fulfilled.

Jeanette (Jetti) Testu

1. BABIES, BOMBS, AND BOOZE: MY CHILDHOOD

Life was good for me until about the age of three, when my parents brought home the first of what was eventually going to add up to seven siblings. Yes, when little Terrence with the long eyelashes arrived, bundled in the family's traditional baptismal gown, I had my first major life realization: the party was over. I can still remember him lying in his crib in the living room of our two-story West Seattle house. Mom, Dad, both sets of grandparents, and various aunts and uncles were all gathered around making their respectful oohs and ahhs while I observed unnoticed from the dining room. For the first time I experienced what it meant to be alone in the world. With six more kids to deal with during my childhood, my parents would never again be able to give me the full attention that I yearned for.

One day, not long after Terrence's arrival, my mother and I went shopping at the local market. While I was underfoot she dropped a jar of pickles on me, and I started howling.

"What's the matter, little boy?" asked a kind woman in the aisle.

"Pickles on head!" I sobbed. I didn't know it then, but the first noble truth of Buddhism—life is suffering—had just hit me over the head.

The Testu family line runs back to seventeenth-century France, where the first known Testu was Claude Guillaume Testu, Marquis de Balincourt, a military marshal and nobleman. As the story goes, a fur trader by the name of Testu traveled down from Quebec along the Mississippi, leaving in his wake a trail of small Testus. When the Testus met the Irish, a flood of Kennedys, Kellehers, O'Briens, Ryans, and Downeys came into the picture. By the time they got to me, I was one-quarter French, three-quarters Irish, and as time would later prove, one hundred percent alcoholic.

My favorite Testu was my dad's mom, Jeanette, a tall, elegant woman who lived in a castle-like house on the cliffs of West Seattle. We visited her on Thanksgiving, Christmas, and other holidays. Jeanette always greeted me with a hug and a smooch, put her arm around me, and walked me sweetly around the house. Her hugs were the only ones I got as a kid, so they meant a lot. I always liked to see the photograph on the mantle that showed Jeanette with her arm around Washington State Governor Rossellini. Then Grandma and I would stop at the picture window in her living room and stare across Elliot Bay at downtown Seattle, and she'd ask me how things were going. After all the cousins, aunts, and uncles arrived, we'd spread out a big potluck dinner, and if it was Thanksgiving, my dad carved the bird.

Jeanette was a state representative for the West Seattle district, and held her office for twenty years. She was also a pro-tem Speaker of the House, honorary sheriff of King County, and on the committee that put together the 1962 Seattle World's Fair. Her spouse was Grandpa Homer, a gentleman loved by all and understood by few except those who frequented the taverns of West Seattle. Homer, a Montana cowboy at heart, was always dragging home unshaven tavern denizens to live in the basement and supposedly help with the cooking. Seems like all they did, though, was smoke cigarettes, drink, and hang around.

My dad, Joseph Kirk Testu, pretty much raised himself. He spent a lot of time in the gully below the house, where he pulled pranks like convincing his friends to test his famous trans-neighborhood rope swing. In 1942 he graduated from Seattle University with a degree in business, and then found his lifelong job at Kenworth Truck Company, first as an engineer, then as a salesman.

My mother, Virginia, was a Kennedy, a vital and beautiful brunette. Her grandparents came to America from Ireland and settled in Kent Valley, just south of Seattle, where they ran a farm on the banks of the Green River. Once a month her grandpa walked thirty miles into Seattle's skid row to get workers for his fields. In exchange for their labor, he offered them no money: just room, board, and all the tobacco they could smoke. By the end of one month they'd all have wandered off, and he'd be ready for a fresh group. When he died, Mom said, his collie howled for days.

Mom had seven brothers and sisters, so I suppose it was natural for her to start building a large family, and that's exactly what she did. Joe and Virginia married, bought a house in West Seattle, and started reproducing.

As more and more siblings appeared, Terrence and I had to move upstairs into an old room with one single window at the far end. My bunk was against one wall; his, the other. Every three years or so my mom gave birth to another kid. During a twenty-year period she produced Timothy Joseph, Terrence Robert, Kathleen Marie, Kirk Patrick, Matthew Julius, Mary Jo, and Mark John. Later on my parents took in another child, a girl named Virginia, so we became eight in total. Good Catholics that they were, my folks enrolled us "spoiled brats," as they liked to call us, in parochial schools. I attended West Seattle's Holy Rosary.

Trouble became me from a young age, and most of the behavioral problems that would plague me for life were already evident by the time I was nine. By the fourth grade, the pattern was set: I did well in school but constantly got in trouble during my off-hours. Some of it was harmless: one time, for instance, I went begging door-to-door for food while my friends observed with great respect from the bushes. On another occasion the same friends and I held an impromptu carnival in our backyard. My offering was to sit cross-legged inside a doghouse acting as a yogi who could answer any question.

But then there was my "unpredictable" side. I'd pull fire alarms, poke bobby pins in electrical outlets, or steal from my neighbors' vegetable gardens. At an early age I learned how to push my mother's buttons—I had a habit of pilfering money from her purse—and she'd yell, "You kids are going to drive me crazy!" She said it so often it developed a melody of its own, and I derived a simple pleasure in getting her to spout it. Why? I had no idea—the reasons behind my behavior were just as much a mystery to me as they were to my parents, and it always meant a struggle between us whenever I was caught doing something crazy.

One boring Saturday afternoon when I was nine or ten, I remember I tossed a very large rock into the open door of a delivery truck as it rumbled down the alley where we lived. The driver skidded to a stop, jumped out, and grabbed me by the scruff of the neck and the seat of the pants. Fuming with anger, he asked me where my house was. I pointed to the home of my friend, Nicholas King, who lived on the other side of the alley. Holding me firmly, the driver knocked on the Kings' back door. When Mrs. King answered, the driver yelled, "Your son just threw a rock into my van!"

Mrs. King looked shocked. "That's not my son. That's the Testu boy! He lives across the alley." The driver dragged me to my real home, where he related the incident to my mother. Mom thanked the driver and then sent me upstairs to wait for my father, who was still at work. When Dad finally got to my room he was hopping mad.

"Get over by the wall!" he yelled as he pulled all the shoes out of the closet, lining them up next to him by the far wall. Still just a small boy, I stood trembling near the opposite wall, where my bedroom's lone window admitted gray light from Seattle's overcast sky.

"Why did you do it?" he yelled as he flung a large boot at me.

"I don't know!" I cried as I tried to dodge the boot. It hit me in the arm.

"What possessed you to do this horrible thing?" He threw a shoe to punctuate each question.

"I don't know!" I cried. More shoes came flying; I sobbed and screamed.

"What goes through your mind when you do these things?"

"I don't know, Dad!" One by one he threw the whole pile of shoes at me, and I answered most of his questions with "I don't know!"

I really didn't know. I was self-aware enough, though, to realize for the first time that Dad probably had a point—why *would* anyone in their right mind throw a rock into a delivery truck? Dad left me confined to the room without dinner to think about what I had done. I solaced myself with deep blanket therapy and cups of tears, and I thought and thought. By the time I was done thinking that night, I had decided something about myself: there must be something terribly wrong with me. I just didn't know what it was.

After my fourth year at Holy Rosary, our family moved to the south end of Seattle to a suburb called Seahurst, which consisted of two gas stations, a candy shop, an old-fashioned meat market cum grocery store, and Saint Francis of Assisi, the local Catholic church and grade school. Dad had just been promoted at Kenworth and was selling trucks all along the West Coast.

At Saint Francis I was now under the tutelage of Sister Superior and the Dominican nuns, who took over my religious training with fervor. I came to believe in a long-haired God that I imagined stood one hundred feet tall. Draped in long white robes, He lived in heaven, which was somewhere up in the sky. I was taught to pray to Jesus when I was troubled, which I often was. (I found that praying actually worked; it seemed to ease my worried mind.) I learned about souls, too. Mine, the nuns explained, was a hazy sphere about nine inches in diameter, located deep inside my midsection. If I committed venial sins, it would get covered with black dots similar to measles. If I died with these spots unpurged, I'd descend to purgatory, where I'd undergo mild torture until my sphere became clear again, and then I'd become eligible for eternity in heaven. A mortal sin, such as missing mass on Sunday or entering the church of some other religion, would create a "grievous offense," and my soul would become black as ink. If I died in that condition, I'd spend eternity roasting in hell.

To up my chances of admission to heaven—because at that point I was pretty concerned that those chances were low—I became an altar boy and learned by heart all the Latin responses to the mass. I was issued a cassock and assigned a mass to perform every Sunday. I enjoyed being on stage in such a theatrical production, and I especially liked enunciating the divine Latin prose just as it had been voiced for thousands of years. I even understood the translations: "I will go unto the altar of God, to God who gave joy to my youth. We praise thee, we bless thee, we adore thee, we give thee thanks for thy great benefits. O Lord God, Heavenly King, God the Father Almighty . . ."

Saint Francis parish had three priests. The pastor was Father Quik, who, true to his name, always said mass in twenty short minutes. (The other two, Fathers Daly and Dooly, took forty minutes each.) Father Quik's true interest in life, it seemed, was salmon fishing out on the ocean at Westport. To help him bring in the catch, he bought a twenty-foot boat with a trailer, and to pull it—believe it or not—a garishly pink, 1957 Lincoln convertible with huge, shark-like fins. But the thing that Father Quik owned that was of far greater interest to me and my classmates was his bullwhip, because when Sister Superior was unable to enforce discipline, she'd ask Father Quik into the schoolyard to take care of matters, and it was never pretty.

Here's just one story. There was a guy in my class named Frank Kemp. Frank was cool: he wore his pants low, his collar up just like Elvis Presley, and he was the first in our school to overtly wear his hair in a DA—a "duck's ass," which we weren't allowed to say, let alone wear. That's just what it looked like, though: hair swept back along the sides and then feathered together real nasty in the back. The DA style was strictly forbidden, but Frank was an expert at wearing his hair. When the nuns weren't around, he'd have it in the full DA position, with us boys in awe and the girls going wild. When the nuns came near, he'd restyle it on the fly with a few deft strokes of his handy pocket comb.

One day during recess, however, Frank got caught with his hair in a full

DA. Sister Superior called in Father Quik, who captured poor Frank in the middle of the playground. While all students from first through eighth grade watched in terror, our benevolent pastor, our compassionate leader of the flock, whipped Frank severely. The sharp crack of the bullwhip could be heard all around Seahurst, and each time the long, thin, leather tail wrapped around Frank's legs, he fell to the ground screaming in agony. These were the types of incidents that color my memory of grade school.

But even the threat of brutal punishments wasn't enough to stop me from endlessly acting out. I felt compelled to put wax paper in people's sandwiches at lunchtime or squeeze my buddies' chests and make them pass out in line at recess. Outside of class, I raised more hell: one time my friends and I stole bullets from the local sporting goods store, then broke into a house that was under construction, found an empty paint can, started a fire in it, and dumped the bullets in. We were so naive that we stood behind narrow two-by-fours as stray bullets whizzed by.

I displayed a wild, neurotic energy and constantly sought attention; even when I could have gotten away scot-free, I couldn't help but take credit for my misdeeds. When I was in seventh grade, my teacher, Sister Angela Marie, had us fill out questionnaires about everyone in the class. They asked us to name the person of the opposite sex we liked the most and the least, and who we thought was the most handsome, popular, or sexiest. She made us sign the papers and turn them in so she could "get to know us better." We never heard another word about those papers, but I felt shamed and violated by her invasion of our privacy. Luckily, I got my chance for revenge. A few weeks later, on an excursion to downtown Seattle's skid road, I happened upon a joke store, where from the vast array of gags and tricks I found one sure to do the job on Sister Angela Marie: a powerful, triple-effect, yellow sulfur, whistling, exploding, spark plug–ignited automobile bomb.

The next day during recess, my friend Mitchell and I ducked out and wired up the bomb to the coil wires of the nuns' station wagon. Sister

Angela was normally the driver. By sheer chance, that afternoon she was taking a flock of visiting nuns out to the Seattle-Tacoma airport. It was our luck that the highest Dominican nun on the entire West Coast was with her—the Mother of our Sister Superior—the Mother of all Mothers, for Christ's sake! All in all, nine nuns loaded into the wagon, and Sister Angela hit the starter. First came the siren scream, then the loud report of the bomb; then the entire car disappeared behind a thick cloud of yellow smoke. All traffic at the little intersection of Seahurst, Washington, ground to a halt as everyone stopped to stare. Suddenly, from out of the smoke and fumes, Sister Angela Marie appeared. Furiously brushing off her robes, she ran like a rocket for several hundred yards, then stopped and appeared to think for a minute. Maybe she was praying for guidance. Abruptly, as if God had given her instructions, she turned on a dime and dashed back to the car, reached in, and gallantly set the emergency brake, although the car was on level ground. All four doors flew open, and the rest of the nuns bailed out. Someone lifted the hood and pointed to the expired bomb hanging from the distributor. My friend and I quietly grabbed our bikes and hit the road.

One week later, while passing Sister Angela in the hall, I said, "Well, Sister, I hear someone put a bomb in your car!" An hour later Sister Superior stormed into our class.

"Testu and Mitchell," she screamed, "I want to see you in the library immediately!" In the library, a small room alongside our class, Sister Superior was waiting, her face twisted with rage. "Did you put the bomb in the nuns' car?" she bellowed.

The two of us replied simultaneously: Mitchell said "Yes!" and I said "No!"

"Which one of you is lying?"

We both pointed at each other and yelled, "He is!"

"That's enough of your lies! Roll up your pants." We pulled our pants up above the calves. From the depths of her robes Sister produced a short, cat-tailed leather whip and started wailing on our hairless little legs. We cried for mercy, but she kept at it, and when she finished our legs were covered with bright red welts.

I was sobbing when I got my mother on the phone. "Mom," I cried, "I put a b-b-bomb in the nuns' station wagon."

My mom couldn't figure out what I was talking about and started laughing. Sister grabbed the phone. "Mrs. Testu, this is not funny. Do you know what your son did? He put a bomb in the nuns' car!"

I took a break from causing trouble—well, purposeful trouble—in the eighth grade, when I noticed that some of the girls in school were becoming quite attractive. Unlike some of the other guys, however, I was terminally shy, and found it extremely difficult to talk to girls about anything, much less tell them how I felt.

To help us develop social skills, the nuns took it upon themselves to hold weekly sock hops in the gymnasium. Every Friday afternoon, in the bright light of day, they assembled the seventh and eighth grade and lined us up, minus shoes, boys against the west wall, girls against the east. (The nuns, especially Sister Angela Marie, observed with great interest from center court.) Sister Superior called them out: "All right, this is a song by Paul Anka, a slow one, and it's men's choice." Then came the hundred-foot walk across the floor to the girls' line. To be first took incredible guts, but then you'd have your choice of girls. The best strategy, I found, was to dash in right after the first guys made their move, running quickly in the middle of the pack, and then at the last second, leaping out for the best beauty as if by accident. Once the choice was made, you were suddenly in the arms of a member of the opposite sex and touching chest to chest. We stepped on each other's feet, made faces over our partners' shoulders, and steered the girls around like we were driving Mercury sedans.

Maybe the sock hops helped, because it was also in eighth grade when I worked up enough nerve to ask out a girl for the first time. I picked Joan.

Joanie was not my favorite girl, mind you, but one I felt reasonably assured would say yes to my request. And she did. One fine summery Saturday, together with my friend Furd and *his* date, we found ourselves taking the bus to Playland, a huge amusement park in the north end of Seattle. I was nervous, but it was a glorious day outside, the park full of Seattleites happily enjoying themselves, and eventually I calmed down. Joan and I lunched on hot dogs, fries, and strawberry milkshakes, then strolled around to check out the exhibits. In one booth we saw through a glass window a live image of a gypsy woman with only half a body. Sure, it was only an illusion created by mirrors and glass, but I didn't care; I was really enjoying Joan's company, and everything was starting to seem magical.

After lunch I bought a roll of tickets and we went on some rides. The roller coaster was an absolute blast; Joan even gave me her hand during one of the tight turns. Then we rode the rocket ship, a bullet-shaped projectile that turned us upside down and emptied the change from my pockets. Next came the Killer Octopus, a giant wheel with five spokes. At the end of each spoke spun two little buckets, each with seats for five people. We shared our gondola with Furd and his date. Once full, the Octopus slowly rolled around, stretching its tentacles, the giant wheel spinning faster and faster. Suddenly the operator tilted the platform into the air at a sharp angle and cranked up the speed. My stomach felt sick. Our buckets were free to rotate in their own orbits around each other, so we began spinning wildly at thrice the speed of the main wheel, racing around like a crankshaft inside an engine. People screamed; the big wheel kept turning faster and faster. My stomach couldn't take it anymore. All at once, I projectile vomited massive quantities of half-digested hot dog, strawberry shake, and fries. Joan, Furd, and his date all tried to block the viscous spray with their hands but were smothered with huge globules of the icky, sticky, pink puke. Pandemonium broke out below as the crowd ran screaming from the falling chunks. Only when my stomach was completely emptied did the big wheel grind to a halt.

Joan and I rode home together on the bus, but little was said. I couldn't even look at her. It was understood we would never go out again, and in fact I didn't try again with a girl until I learned how to drink a year later.

Upon graduation from St. Francis, I advanced to O'Dea, the same Catholic preparatory school for boys my father graduated from in 1936. O'Dea's faculty were the tough and inspired Christian Brothers of Ireland, an elite teaching order of Catholic monks who kept vows of poverty, chastity, and obedience. O'Dea had no frills: no metal, wood, or auto shops, and of course, no girls.

Teaching was the brothers' lives, their daily offering to God, and they taught with fire and passion. Many, like Brother Farrell, my English composition teacher, were quite eloquent. He delivered his speeches like a Shakespearean actor, using the language with a precision and force I'd never experienced. He'd start out speaking in a normal tone, obviously enjoying the way his mind found the most choice and powerful word combinations. As he talked, he strode briskly up and down the aisles, his long black robes brushing near each of us. Walking and talking, he gradually raised the volume and force of his voice, ending up by roaring so loud the windows rattled while we all sat bolt upright, frozen in our seats. After a moment of silence, he'd drop his voice to a raspy whisper and summarize his speech in a few concise sentences while we strained forward to hear every word he uttered. Once finished with his masterful delivery, he'd often twirl around, his robes fanning out like a Sufi dancer, put his face directly in front of mine, and ask, "Isn't that right, Mr. Testu?"

All the brothers carried black leather straps that measured one foot long by two inches wide by half an inch thick. These formidable weapons weighed about a pound each. Punishment was doled out in sets of three: one shot on each hand and a whack on the butt. In accordance with the severity of a boy's crime, he got two, two, and two, or five, five, and five, and so forth. One day I got caught making bird noises in the classroom.

Brother Farrell stood me in front of the room and told me to hold out my hands for a beating. I braced myself as Brother wound up for a big strike. He made a sweeping revolution of his arm, bringing the strap down toward my quivering flesh with the force of a freight train. At the last millisecond, however, I withdrew my hand, and he missed, lost his balance, and crashed to the floor. The class erupted with laughter, but Brother, once he dusted himself off, got in his whacks in double measure.

During my freshman year a form of gambling became very popular on the playground. Every day at noon we'd gather in the alley behind school to pitch coins. If your coin landed closest to the wall, you got to keep all the money. Every day more people quit playing sports and took up gambling. I suppose it was only a matter of time until we were caught, but it still came as a surprise to us when one day Brother King came out, blew his referee's whistle, and brought recess to a halt. Hearing his shrill alarm, more brothers poured out of the building, and together they quickly lined us boys up in a row stretching from one end of the field to the other. They ordered everyone to hold out their hands. Then, with fiery intent, they walked the line, strapping our hands. When they reached the end, they made us bend over and touch our toes, and with sixty young butts facing skyward, they ran the line again, leather straps lashing furiously.

Looking back, I wonder what would have happened, if instead of beating me, the good brothers would have said, "Mr. Testu, it seems to me you're having problems paying attention in class. Why don't you do us both a favor and go down and see the counselor?" But there was no counseling back then, for me or for anybody—which was unfortunate, because my problems were just growing worse.

In sophomore year, for instance, it became required for me to take phys ed. I was the youngest in the class, so I hadn't physically matured like the rest of the guys. They all had pubic hairs, and I had none. There was just this tiny pecker about the size of a Virginia Peanut, and a scrumpy little shriveled-up set of balls. I was tall and a good basketball player, so I did OK

during the actual gym period, but I was terrified of the mandatory showers that followed it. I'd go up to the dimly lit balcony where we dressed
and fiddle around with my locker while everyone else showered. Quickly
undressing, I'd pretend to dry myself off—facing the locker, of course—
and then hop into my clothes as if I had showered. I didn't understand
that everything would appear in its own time, and I'd soon be normal just
like everyone else. In the meantime my lack of self-esteem bludgeoned me
into social silence.

I needed help: someone to talk to, someone to listen to me. But I was
lost, scared, and confused, and I didn't know how to ask for it. We were
taking college preparatory courses that someone had deemed best for us,
but no one was showing us how to piece it all together. Maybe the brothers assumed that the parents were giving counsel, helping to make plans
and choices, and perhaps most parents were. But mine weren't. I had no
idea who I was, what I was doing, or—now that it was time to think about
these things—where I was going.

I was fourteen when I discovered alcohol. One night, Furd stole a bottle
of Old Overholt, a kind of whiskey, from his father's liquor cabinet, and a
bunch of us neighborhood guys took it down to a sandpit near our houses
and got drunk. One of us, Doozer, became violently sick and passed out
in a pool of his own puke. I was dizzy myself. But I also instantly knew I'd
found a true friend in the bottle—someone who warmed me deep inside
and who took away all my fears and pain.

From that day on, I drank whenever I got the chance. I had never
developed real social skills and was crippled by insecurity, especially around
girls, so consuming massive quantities of alcohol became a prerequisite for
anything extracurricular. It took the edge off, filling me with false courage.
When I had alcohol, I never felt like there was anything wrong with me;
I finally had an identity—and it was one that I liked. My motto became
"Get drunk and be somebody."

I began stealing booze from my parents' liquor cabinet regularly. When they were gone I'd pour a little from each bottle into a Mason jar and replace what I took with water. My dad was a daily drinker, so there was always a fresh supply. To supplement the alcohol, I started smoking Marlboros and immediately became addicted. I lived for my smokes and those times I could get drunk. While most of my friends turned mellow and tired when we drank, I got wild.

I started skipping school. With my stolen jar of booze, I'd go to the Green Parrot Theater in Seattle and watch old movies all afternoon, or wander around downtown, investigating tall buildings. Occasionally I'd "borrow" other people's cars and take them on high-speed joy rides. (I'd always return them to within a block of where I had taken them, if possible.)

One day during the beginning of my junior year, on a total impulse, a friend I called Hazelnuts and I decided to drop out of school and head for California. Our plan was to hitchhike to San Francisco, get a ship, and go to sea, although I'm not sure what we were planning to do once we got there. We got on the freeway ramp, stuck out our thumbs, and before we could think twice, were heading south. The weather quickly turned to rain and we had very little money, but we survived by eating Snickers bars and sleeping in abandoned cars. We made it to San Francisco in three days. The money, though, ran out soon after our arrival, and since we were too scared to seek work we decided to head home. In Oregon a policeman stopped us, ran a check, and threw us in jail as runaways. The next day both of our fathers, who had never met before, picked us up, and we all rode home together in an embarrassed, stony silence. At one point my dad asked, "Tim, I just have one question. Why did you do it?" Nothing had changed in a decade of my life: I still didn't know the answer.

When we got back to Seattle my dad went up to O'Dea and talked the brothers into giving me one more chance. Since he was an honored alumnus, I was readmitted. My behavioral problems persisted, however, and by the middle of my junior year I was permanently expelled.

I enrolled in the public high school, where I concentrated further on my drinking. In the span of one year I was involved in crashing my friend's father's car by (accidentally) driving it over a cliff, stole my own father's car, and landed in jail again when the cops broke up a party I had driven to with a car my parents didn't know I had bought. It was no wonder that I did not graduate in 1962 with the rest of my class. Instead, I had to return for an extra semester and ended up graduating, all by myself, in the class of 1962 and a half.

2. IN TROUBLE DEEP: MY TIME IN THE NAVY

The very same afternoon that I graduated high school, I drove to the local recruiting center. Maybe I was motivated by my failed attempt to find a life at sea—I don't know. I hadn't made any plans for college and at the time a life in the navy seemed just as good as any other.

The recruiter's office was small and windowless and located in the back of the building. I walked in and saw a sailor, probably about thirty, stretched back in his chair with his arms behind his head and feet up on the desk. Wearing a tight blue uniform decked out with tons of medals and decorations, he looked just like Jack Nicholson in *The Last Detail*. "I'd like to learn about the navy," I said.

"Great!" he replied as he stood, grinned, and shook my hand. "My name is Ed Ferrari. Why don't you shut and lock the door, grab a seat there, and we'll get down to business?"

I locked the door and sat on a folding chair next to his desk as he reached into his lower desk drawer and produced a six-pack of Olympia beer. We sat together and drank two each as he told me about his experiences on the USS *Stickleback*, a submarine that had sunk during peacetime training exercises a few years back.

"Yeah," he said, "I was there in '58 when she went down. It was real scary. We were coming up to periscope depth from down deep, and apparently the sonar man was asleep or something, because we didn't hear the screws of the destroyer, and he rammed us amidships. His bow cut into us like a knife, knocking the hydraulic manifold in the control room off the bulkhead. I swear we could read the depth markings painted on his hull."

Nobody actually died when the USS *Stickleback* sank, but in the dramatic retelling Ferrari proceeded to treat me to, half of the crew had perished in an action-packed rescue attempt, and he had watched the submarine's rooms fill with water one by one until the boat slowly sank under the waves, taking his friends with it. Mr. Ferrari had my full attention, and he knew it.

"You know," he continued nonchalantly, "I think you'd really like subs. The chow is the best in the navy, and they have an open icebox policy—anytime you're hungry you just help yourself. Plus, you get hazardous duty pay. And the rules are not as strict as in the surface navy; there's a special kind of camaraderie among the crew. Most of the people don't even display their rank or ratings, and everyone talks to each other on a first-name basis."

He paused to check and see if I was still with him. I was. "You know," he said again, as he popped the tops off of two more beers, "I have a program here that you'll love—the nuclear power program. You'll have to sign up for six years, but if you can pass the entrance test, we'll send you to all kinds of schools, including nuclear power school, which alone is equivalent to two years of college. Here's how it works: First you go to boot camp, and then an 'A' school, where you'll learn a specific trade, like electronics, radios, or turbines. Then you'll go aboard an operating submarine for six months, until you get qualified in submarines and earn your silver dolphins, which is like earning your wings. After that you'll go to nuclear power school, and then on to a nuclear prototype plant on dry land for six months. If you graduate from all of these, you'll be assigned to either a fast attack or a fleet ballistic missile sub. What do you think?"

"Wow!" I exclaimed, looking longingly at the silver dolphins pinned on his uniform. "Do you think I'm eligible for all of that?"

"We'll see. I'm going to send you to our main office in Seattle, where you'll take some tests. When I get the results, I'll call you, and we'll take it from there."

I went to Seattle to take the tests. Because I never studied in school, I was never considered to be a "good" student, but I was bright (when I was sober, anyway) and it helped me especially that I had always had a love of all things mechanical. I used to like going into my dad's shop and borrowing his tools to build things. (He kept the shop locked, so I had to wait until he was gone before unscrewing the hinges from the door and removing it, but that's neither here nor there.) When I was in middle school I built a miniature hydroplane to tow behind my bicycle; a couple years later I put together a wooden soapbox racer powered by a lawn mower engine that featured foot steering and a homemade clutch rigged out of an automobile emergency brake. So the navy's mechanical tests were easy for me, and when I returned to the recruiting center in a couple of days, Mr. Ferrari had good news.

"Mr. Testu," he exclaimed, "You have the highest scores of just about anyone who's been down there! You'll have no problem getting into the nuclear program and on subs."

Without a moment of hesitation, I took the pen Ferrari offered me and signed away six years of the prime of my life. Just a few days after that, I was on a plane to boot camp in San Diego.

When I arrived at the naval training center, I was greeted by the sight of hundreds of mattresses drying in the hot California sun. The center had just suffered an epidemic of spinal meningitis, and several recruits had already died. It was a stark, depressing way to begin, and my nervous feelings only got worse as my first day kicked into gear. My head was shaved and my civilian clothes mailed home. Now looking like a proper recruit, I was sent to a company led by a macho commander named Mr. Allard.

Every single day for the next two months, Allard drilled and marched us for several hours on the hot blacktop fields appropriately named "grinders," where it wasn't uncommon to see recruits pass out and fall down from heat exhaustion. It wasn't easy marching in unison, and even when most of us got things right, there were always one or two who screwed things up for the whole company. Each morning all sixty of us stood at attention on the marching field for inspection. Mr. Allard, who was really nothing more than a first-class seabee—equivalent to a buck sergeant in the army—then inspected us for cleanliness and proper uniforms. One day, he stopped in front of me and ordered me to take off my white hat. He looked at the rim where it folds up.

"Testu, this white hat is filthy," he yelled. "It isn't fit for a pig." I looked at the hat. There was an almost imperceptible yellow ring around the edge—we weren't allowed to use bleach. "In fact, you *are* a pig, Testu!" he raved as he threw the hat out on the grinder. "I want you to get down on your hands and knees and crawl around."

For a microsecond I thought about my options. I'd heard about the special barracks they kept for people who didn't do as they were told, the infamous "4809" where young recruits were held back from graduation, locked up, and tortured by the most sinister and evil of men. The horror stories that filtered back from there were enough to curdle your blood. I decided to do as he said: I got down on the ground.

"OK, Testu, I want you to say, 'Oink, oink, I'm a pig!'"

"Oink, oink," I mumbled quietly. Hot blood of embarrassment and humiliation spread across my face.

"That's not loud enough!" Allard screamed.

"Oink, oink, I'm a pig!" I yelled as I stared into the harsh texture of the blacktop. Finally he allowed me to retrieve my hat and stand as he gave a long lecture on how we needed to scrub our hats until they were white as white could be. I stared at my hat. I just wanted to crawl inside of it and die.

The fear of failing inspections like that one was so intense that we recruits sometimes turned against each other in order to pass. There were "blanket parties," where guys got up in the middle of the night and threw a blanket over the recruit that was causing the company to fail and beat the pulp out of him. In this peculiar manner, we learned how to function as a team and look out for each other. Gradually the time slipped by.

There is one day everyone loves in boot camp, and that is graduation day. The navy's personal plan for me, as Mr. Ferrari had first outlined, was machinist's mate school, then submarine school in New London, Connecticut. After that I'd go to a conventional (diesel-powered) submarine for about six months, giving me time to "qualify" in submarines and earn the silver dolphins. Then it was nuclear power school for six months, after that a land-based, nuclear prototype for another six months, and then, finally, I'd report to a real nuclear sub.

Machinist's mate school was a breeze, partly because of the generous seventy-two-hour passes we got on weekends to leave the base and do whatever we pleased until Monday morning. What pleased me was always the same: buy booze, get drunk, and be somebody. For two months, I guzzled manhattans in Manhattan, slurped sloe gin fizzes in the Bronx, and shot ten-cent beers in Spanish Harlem. Sub school was similarly simple, and I sailed through without much trouble.

After sub school, my orders were to report aboard the USS *Rock*, a diesel-electric World War II sub out of San Diego. The weather was hot and sunny as I found my way to Point Loma, a peninsula on the western reach of town that provided a safe harbor for Submarine Flotilla One. I showed my orders to the gate guard and slowly drove down the hill to the piers. When I reached the parking lot, I could see a couple of submarine tenders, huge gray ships about the size of a cruise vessel. One was tied to the pier, the other anchored in the harbor. Tied up next to each was a "nest" of four or five submarines. The *Rock* was the last one out from the pier. I took a long time looking at her: my new home.

I walked out to the boat, eager to settle in and get acquainted with my shipmates. The topside watch directed me down the hatch, where I descended into the crew's mess. Two boat chiefs and a big first-class torpedoman were sitting in the crowded little space drinking coffee. "What's your name?" asked the big torpedoman.

"Testu," I replied.

"No, no. What's your first name?" I couldn't believe this. Here I was, fresh out of boot camp, more or less, and already a first-class petty officer wanted to relate to me on a first-name basis. Ferrari had been right!

"Tim," I answered cheerfully.

"Well, fuck you, Tim!" he said, and both he and the chiefs burst into laughter.

Turning crimson red, I scrambled from the room.

The main difference between subs and surface craft is that on a submarine everyone's life is always on the line. If a valve or pipe were to burst, the boat would flood and sink before anyone could escape. By 1962, the navy had already lost two nuclear subs, the *Thresher* and the *Scorpion*, and those had been built with the latest in high-tech materials and safeguards. Imagine the possibilities for sinking in a twenty-five-year-old sub like the *Rock*, with thousands of ancient valves and a banged-up hull that had been used and abused for two and a half decades.

To compensate for all the danger, submariners go through a rigorous, six-month qualification program. Each newcomer must intimately learn every compartment and system on the ship. He must know how to do not only his own job, but everyone else's, too, and must be able to respond to any emergency throughout the boat. For example, a radarman would have to demonstrate in the control room all the complicated procedures for surfacing the ship. Until you became qualified, you were treated as "lower than whaleshit" and, regardless of rank or rate, were looked down upon by the qualified crew—this was the unwritten law of survival in submarines.

During my first three weeks on the boat, we partook in war games off the Mexican coast with surface vessels from the US Navy. I worked in the galley as a messman, washing dishes and waiting on the crew, and trying not to show my unparalleled terror as the sub dove, surfaced, and snorkeled throughout the long hours of the day and night. I couldn't stand up straight at the sink because of the curve of the hull, and the deck was constantly covered with slippery sweat. Every time we dove, tilting down toward the bottom of the ocean, I feared the worst.

I slept in the stern room with thirty-five other men, my bunk the bottom of a stack of five. It stank in there. I was 6'4" and the bunks were only six feet, so my feet extended onto the pillow of Radioman Snyder. When the guy above me, Torpedoman Rheo, crawled into his kip, his springs brushed my belly. If I wanted to turn over, I had to slide out into the aisle, roll over, then slide back in.

The rest of the sub was no more spacious: twenty-eight feet at her widest point. The hull was divided into a series of nine compartments, one after the other. First was the forward torpedo room, where various kinds of torpedoes, or "fish," were lashed to the bulkheads; then the forward battery room, where 125 tons of batteries were stored. Aft of the battery room came the radar and sonar room; then the control room, which contained the diving station; the after battery room, which had the crew's mess and more berthing space; the forward and after engine rooms, where four 1600-horsepower diesel-generator sets were stored; then the maneuvering room; and finally, the stern room.

During my last week of mess cooking, the chief of the boat informed me I'd soon be going to work in the engine rooms. As a novice, nonqualified "fireman"—what the navy calls those in the engineering track—I worked on machinery during the day and on my qualifications at night. When the vessel was in port, we engineers overhauled the engines, spreading all their thousands of parts out on the main deck. Back at sea, the vessel played more war games, which the navy had gone to great lengths to make as realistic as possible. We were pursued by real ships that dropped real depth charges that made real booms and, shaking the boat, knocked out very real light bulbs. We shot real torpedoes, but without the explosive warheads—they were set to not hit the surface ships, but to run a few feet under them. We acted as both hunter and hunted.

The thrill of submerging the boat never wore off. We'd be steaming along at about twenty knots, all four engines running full blast, belching out hot black smoke, and the captain would call the bridge over the announcing system and order, "Officer of the deck, this is the captain. Submerge the boat!" The officer on deck would yell, "Clear the bridge!" and take one last sweeping look around before he rang the klaxon twice and quickly followed the two lookouts down the hatch. Throughout the boat we'd hear the sound, "Ahhoooooooogah, Ahhoooooooogah!"

At the same moment, the chief of the watch in the control room pulled all the levers on the hydraulic manifold, venting off air in the ballast tanks. Shuddering and shaking violently, the boat tilted down, thrusting her way into the sea. Meanwhile, back in the engine rooms all hell would be breaking loose—the throttleman leaping from his bench, jumping back and forth, throwing levers, shutting valves, and trying to get the engines shut down. He had about twenty-nine different things to do in sixty seconds, and if he muffed anything, the boat would sink. My job was to help him, and to shut by hand the huge gate valves that backed up the quick-closing hydraulic units. In the maneuvering room, the electricians were throwing big switches, shifting the load from the diesel generators to the batteries, and ringing up full speed so the boat would get down quickly. (The navy had learned from its war experience that when it is time to dive, you don't mess around; you get down fast so no one can hit you.)

Meanwhile, in the control room, the lookouts would be taking over the bow and stern planes and tilting them into the full-dive position. All during this period, the chief of the watch would be nervously eyeing the "Christmas tree," a panel of red and green lights—a red light indicating, for example, that a hatch was open. If all the lights didn't turn green within sixty seconds, we'd have to emergency surface. When the boat reached a predetermined depth—say, one hundred and fifty feet—the chief would blow the negative tank, expelling about forty tons of excess ballast using thousands of pounds of compressed air. The diving officer would order the bow and stern planes operators to level the vessel off, and back in maneuvering, the electricians would slow down the main propulsion motors. Suddenly it would become so quiet that all you could hear was the creaking sounds of the hull compressing and perhaps the distant sounds of screws as the surface craft above wondered where the hell we were.

I loved being on the sub and worked hard, finishing my qualifications and receiving my silver dolphins in just four and a half months instead of the usual six. But when the boat would pull into San Diego for the weekend, I would completely let loose—and that's an understatement. Anytime I was ashore, I worked hard at keeping a steady stream of booze going down my throat so my alcoholic buzz would never go away. My drinking capacities soon became enormous. I could guzzle double shots all night and still maintain what I thought was my great cool, and I was particularly proud of my ability to drive while under the influence. I quickly developed a reputation among the crew as a party animal. I'm not so sure that I was, though; it was just that it never occurred to me that I could have a good time without drinking. When I was sober I was still afraid to talk to anyone, especially women.

One night, back when I was still washing dishes, I joined a few electricians who were using 190-proof alcohol to clean a generator and mixing the excess fluid with orange juice to make "screwdrivers." I was blitzed before I even left the boat. That night was my first blackout. I awoke the next morning with no memory of anything I did—and a tattoo of a black panther on my right arm. My Uncle Pat had one just like it, a tribute to the Testu family herald, and I must have admired it as a kid. Now I had one, too—for the rest of my life.

It wasn't long before blacking out became routine. Another night I got drunk at the Pump Room, the enlisted men's club on base, and then took the boys out for a joy ride in my Austin Mini Cooper, which my parents had helped me put a down payment on before I had left for the USS *Rock*. I found a road-racing course through a bunch of abandoned streets in the base and drove around and around, faster and faster, the car leaning over and the boys screaming to get out, until finally the base police came along and chased me out. As my bingeing worsened and I spent all of my pay on partying, I was unable to make payments on the Mini. Finally my mother had to fly down to San Diego to get the car and drive it all the way back to the dealer in Seattle. I was a disgrace to my family. But I was just getting started.

I received orders to go to nuclear power school in Vallejo, California, for my intensive six-month course in nuclear theory. This school was very tough; they had courses in metallurgy, physics, and advanced math. I managed to squeak by, though I didn't study much. My focus was on partying with my new friends—drinkers all. One weekend, on yet another bender, this time in Santa Cruz, we rented a room on the beach right next door to a bunch of army guys, who were also throwing a party. It was less than an hour before the inevitable altercation broke out, and the next thing I knew I was incarcerated in the Santa Cruz jail.

The commanding officer of nuclear power school was a rather nice sort. He'd already served a two-year stint as captain of a nuclear sub, and now he was theoretically safe and sound, having only to watch over his flock of boy wonders at nuke school. Besides a warning I had received from a senior officer who had caught me trying to sneak onto the *Rock* as it was preparing to leave the dock, drunk and missing my sailor hat, I had never been reprimanded for behavior, so this was my first formal appearance at a Captain's Mast. I stood at attention in my dress whites, staring down the long boardroom table with its green felt cover. The captain sat at the other end, his scowling executive officer standing next to him.

"Testu, I've looked over your records, and it seems to me you're a good sailor. You've had consistently high marks, and there is no indication of you ever being in trouble." (Little did he know!) "Now, I don't want this one incident to screw up your whole career, so I'm going to simply restrict you to base for the next thirty days, and then we won't have to put anything in your record. Do you understand?"

"Yes, sir!" I gratefully replied, noticing the exec's stern frown of disapproval.

I spent the next thirty days on base, watching a movie every night at the base theater and getting my daily beer fix at the enlisted men's club. When my restriction was up, I felt like I deserved a break from all my good behavior and promptly got plastered at the Horse and Cow, a San Francisco submarine bar whose walls were decorated with all kinds of submarine war paraphernalia. The owner, Loopy, was an old, well-known character who had once run for mayor of San Francisco.

When I walked in, Loopy saw the dolphins on my uniform, blasted the diving alarm, and bought me my first round. He said I could drink all I wanted at the Horse and Cow, and if I ran out of money, he'd run me up a bar bill. With this generous proclamation ringing in my ears, I proceeded to down a massive amount of drinks before walking out into the city. Some guy tried to put the make on me. I ran through a fence; I became someone else. I uprooted trees and shrubs, and blacked out. Hat lost again, I was eventually arrested by the shore patrol.

The next day I reported to Captain's Mast for the second time. It was graduation week, and despite my horrible drinking escapades, I'd managed to make it successfully through the school. A great career lay ahead of me; I even had orders to the coveted nuclear prototype in upstate New York.

"Testu," the old man drawled in a disappointed tone, "I really don't know what to do with you. I've thrown people out of this school for getting parking tickets. I've shitcanned them to the surface fleet for the rest of their enlistment. They'll never see another submarine again. Then I give you a break, and here you are, running around like a complete maniac. What's wrong with you, anyway?"

"I don't know, sir." The exec was livid. I'm sure he was happy to see me going.

"I'm sure you don't. You have a fine record here, and you're all ready to graduate. I just can't believe you'd do something like this. And you know what? I don't feel like dealing with it. I'm going to put your record up on the shelf here, and we're going to be watching you. This is your last chance. If you don't shape up, I'm going to ship you right out of here. It's your decision what happens. Now get back to class."

On the way out, the executive officer couldn't help but snarl at me, "Are you happy, Testu? Do you think the punishment was too stiff?" Well, it certainly would have been if he were at the helm. As it was, I couldn't have dreamed of a better deal. Not only was there no punishment, I wasn't even restricted to base. Ahh! Ain't life great when Jupiter's hanging in midheaven. A guy can do no wrong.

Now at that time, by sheer coincidence, my old boat, the USS *Rock*, had just arrived in Vallejo for a six-month shipyard overhaul, and I had access to all my old buddies. The next day after school I walked out to the dry dock where the *Rock* was already up on blocks. I found one of my friends, Frank Messerli, and we decided to go out and celebrate my recent good fortune with a few drinks. We took a bus across the Carquinez bridge and down into the little town of Crockett, where they didn't check identification (I was still under twenty-one), and we drank for hours. The last thing I remember was being dragged into the alley by a very upset bartender who was threatening to beat me to a pulp. I talked my way out of it, but I did go into a functional blackout—unconscious, but still operating; the lights on but nobody home.

When I next came to consciousness, I found myself at the wheel of a black 1957 Chevrolet Bel Air hardtop, heading south on the freeway toward Oakland. I looked down at the instruments: the gas gauge was on empty, and the car was doing 90 mph. It seemed odd to see my body at the controls of this strange car. Whose car was it? I looked down the column at the ignition switch and saw there was no key in it—this was a model that didn't require a key if the ignition wasn't locked. I somehow felt completely sober.

Suddenly I snapped to it. Holy shit. Did I steal this car? I looked in the rearview mirror and saw a sheriff's vehicle following me with his red lights flashing. How did I get here? I had a vague memory of speeding up an exit ramp, heading into opposing traffic on the freeway, and then crossing over the divider to get going in the right direction. Where was I trying to go? And where was Frank? A shot of adrenaline ran through me as I assessed the situation with all the reason of an utter drunk. "If I pull over now, I'll be in giant trouble for sure. If I punch it, though, at least I'll have a chance of getting away." I went with option B. I accelerated to 120 mph, burying the needle in the stops. All around me cars were doing the speed limit, but I shot past them like they were going backward—it felt more like I was flying an aircraft than driving. Drenched in cold sweat, my body shaking terribly, I ditched the cop.

At the next off-ramp I bailed off the freeway. The yellow signs advised slowing to 30 mph, but I was going 90. Fishtailing in a wild drift, the Chevy flew like a bird over the dividers and down the on-ramp back onto the freeway. Deciding to try it again, I took another off-ramp. This time the brakes faded, and I drifted and spun, sliding to a standstill alongside the road in a cloud of smoke and dust.

No cops were in sight. If I'd had any brains, I would just drive down a back road, hide the car, and run for it. Instead, I fired up the car and sped down a twisting, two-lane country road the universe had just offered up to me. I raced through a red light in a small town, doing over 80 mph. Eventually some cops caught sight of me. Truthfully, I was surprised it took them as long as it did to find me. A state trooper, who could drive every bit as fast as I, hooked up ten feet off my tail, and I couldn't shake him. We drove a couple of miles in a wild and reckless manner at extremely high speeds, crisscrossing through the back streets of rural America.

After a while I began to feel funny in the back of my neck, as if perhaps I were going to receive a bullet there or something. Thinking that it would be best to play it safe, I pulled off to the side of the road. The trooper stopped about thirty feet behind me. In my side mirror I watched him get out of his car and draw his weapon. My body was shaking uncontrollably, and I was overwhelmed with raw, animal fear. "Oh Christ," I said to myself. Spurred by the thought of what would happen if I got caught, I slapped the car into gear, punched the son-of-a-bitch, and roared off with the rear tires spinning wildly in the gravel. I looked in the mirror again. The huge cloud of dust and grit had caused the trooper and his car to disappear. I was still concerned about getting hit by one of his bullets, though, so I scrunched down in the seat and steered with my hand, keeping the pedal to the metal as the Chevy fishtailed wildly up the street. I peeked up every few seconds to straighten us out.

We were doing 100 mph when we reached the crest of a hill, and I realized a few seconds too late that the road had come to an end. I couldn't stop, so I threw the car into a sideways drift and we shot off the road . . . and through someone's yard. In the midst of this dynamic chaos I noticed a 1954 Oldsmobile sitting in the driveway. I didn't want to hit it sideways, so I straightened the Chevy out—and then we hit the Olds. In what seemed like slow motion, it reared up into the air and bent inward like a twisted beer can. There was an enormous shower of sparks; it was raining crunched metal and broken glass as the Chevy caved in like an accordion right up to the dashboard. Together, the two cars smashed into the house, taking out a large corner of one room. Then the whole massive heap of cars and lumber settled, and suddenly there was nothing but silence, broken only by the steady drip, drip, drip of the radiator.

Stunned but unhurt, I bailed out, jumped a fence, ran down the street, and hid in the bushes next to another house. Within seconds, the sound of sirens shook the night air, and cops descended on the place from every direction, running around and shouting orders for the search. They even had dogs looking for me. Sweating and shaking profusely, I was now terribly afraid of getting shot, or worse yet, bit. In yet another spontaneous decision, I crawled out from the bushes, stood on a lit porch, and pretended to be a concerned house owner.

A few of the passing cops glanced at me as I stood there with my arms crossed and kept on running. But there was one guy who came along, stopped, and looked right at me.

"What's going on out there?" I inquired.

He studied me for a second. I thought I had him.

"I'll tell you what's going on," he replied. "You're going to jail!"

I was handcuffed, hauled to the Contra Costa county jail, and arrested for grand theft and thirteen moving violations, which included "evading arrest, doing 120 in a 65, 80 in a 25, running several red lights and stop signs, drunk driving, and driving so as to endanger the lives of the community." Inside the booking office, two deputies, the ones who first started chasing me, shook their heads in amazement. They wanted to know where I learned how to drive so fast.

Still drunk, I proudly replied, "I used to have an Austin Cooper."

I spent three days in jail, the first night in the drunk tank, a stainless steel pit where everyone else was retching and puking. Meanwhile, the high command at nuclear power school set out to rescue me. Not wanting the world at large to know that one of their nuclear plant operators was running amok, they sent a legal officer from the navy to represent me in court. Embellishing only slightly on my impeccable record, he told the judge that I was one of the finest young men the navy had ever enlisted, and I had simply had too much to drink. He also emphasized that the navy would really punish me when the civilian court got through—double jeopardy be damned—so he pleaded they be especially lenient.

The judge dismissed all charges, issued me a meager twenty-five-dollar fine, and put me on ninety days probation. Returning to face the music at nuke school, I figured I'd be court-martialed and sent to Portsmouth Naval Prison. Instead, the captain didn't even want to speak to me. I was booted out of nuclear power school and sentenced to a hearing before the submarine review board to determine if I could ever get back on subs.

Restricted as a "liberty risk" once again, I strolled down to the base chapel one lonely Saturday and saw it was open for confession. I walked in and made a pretty good act of confession. (I didn't go into great detail, but I think I pretty well covered everything.) On Sunday, I partook in the sacraments of mass and Holy Communion. As I returned down the aisle with the host melting on my tongue, I noticed Charles Zekan, commanding officer of the USS *Rock*, sitting in the front pew staring at me. His eyes lit up when he noticed me.

Two days later, the submarine review board convened at base headquarters in Vallejo. The panel consisted of three submarine skippers whose sole purpose was to decide whether nuke dropouts would be allowed to return to submarine duty. It was well known that only one in seven who suffered this grueling interrogation ever got back to subs, so I figured my particular chances were around one in a zillion. When I reported for my dreaded appointment with the review board, a yeoman, the navy's answer to a personal secretary, sat me in a knotty-pine waiting room with three other nervous nuke dropouts, and we talked about what had brought us there. They were having academic problems; I was the only one with behavioral problems. None of us entertained much hope of seeing a submarine again.

After the others had taken their turn, the yeoman led me into a dark, windowless office deep within the bowels of the building. I could barely see, but when my eyes gradually became accustomed to the dark, I could make out the stark outlines of three highly decorated officers gathered around a big oak table—two had their feet up on it. All three were commanding officers of US Navy submarines. I recognized the skipper of the *Bream* and Commander Zekan. Impeccably dressed in my blue wool uniform, I stood at attention as they took turns grilling me. Zekan didn't say much, but the other two were tough. I decided to treat this as just another demanding submarine drill, another chance to show my skill, so I fabricated answers on the fly as best I could. They wanted to know the usual—why I did it, what went through my mind, what was wrong with me—the same old questions my dad used to ask. I told them I didn't know, I wasn't sure, and that it would never happen again. In his lazy Southern drawl the old man off the *Bream* inquired, "Tell me, Testu, why should I have *you* on *my* submarine?"

"Well sir," I replied, "I'm actually quite new to this outfit, and although I've made a few mistakes, I've got a whole lot of good stuff that I haven't done yet. I just need the opportunity to do it all." They all roared with laughter.

"How many chances do you need, Testu?"

"Just one, sir. I'm proud to be a qualified submariner, and I earned my dolphins in record time. I love the diesel boats, and I know 'em like the back of my hand. I belong on subs; I don't think I'm cut out for the surface fleet."

"Yeah, Testu," he snarled, "there are plenty of people out there who want diesel boats, but none of them have been in all the trouble you've been in. That's all; you can go. Dismissed! Get outta here!"

From Mare Island in Vallejo I was sent to the transit barracks at Treasure Island, a tiny naval base situated halfway between San Francisco and Oakland, where I was told to await my permanent orders from the Bureau of Personnel in Washington. The morning of my arrival, the base master at arms assigned me to the marine brig, where I was a "chaser." I would march prisoners to various locations around the base for dental work, psychiatric consultation, and so forth. And if they ran, I was supposed to chase them. Sometimes I had in my tenuous possession ten or eleven of these miserable souls with their shaven heads, gruesome tattoos, and forlorn looks. I don't know what I would have done if they had turned on me or tried to run away, but fortunately none of them seemed inclined. Hell, my crimes were probably worse than theirs. But I was much more concerned about where the navy was going to send me now. I could end up on a garbage scow out of the South Pole.

To help my cause of catching a decent ship, I upped my attendance at mass and continued to go to confession and Holy Communion. (I also enjoyed a few very careful outings to town.) Finally, after two weeks, my orders arrived. Of all the ships in the US Navy, I was to report back to my old boat, the USS *Rock* out of San Diego. My prayers had been answered—either that, or Commander Zekan had spoken up for me.

My return to the *Rock* was a real homecoming: my friends were anxiously waiting for me and grinning at my arrival. I couldn't help but grin myself—I'd beaten the odds once again. In truth, everything I had done, the person I was becoming, disturbed me greatly, but I decided to put it all in the back of my mind. I thanked Commander Zekan for saving me and went about my job in the engine room with renewed fervor.

Our operations took us into the pure, azure waters off the Mexican coast, fifty miles south of San Diego, where we snorkeled, dove, and surfaced. Since I'd become a petty officer, a third-class machinist's mate, they started breaking me in as throttleman of the watch in the forward engine room. There I stood four hours on and eight hours off, around the clock with an oiler to help me out. There was no noise-protection booth; we sat directly on top of monstrous 1100 KW generator sets, just beneath the instrument panel, which we scanned continuously for indications of problems.

In early 1964 we began preparing the *Rock* for a six-month deployment in the western Pacific—or as they called it in naval parlance, a WesPac run. Just prior to departure, Commander Zekan received notice from the flotilla commander that we couldn't operate in WesPac without a certified ship's diver on board. That very day, the skipper posted a notice in the crew's mess asking for volunteers to go to navy diver's school. There were twelve names on the list when I added mine. Two days later, I was picked. Thus, on the same day that the *Rock* sailed for her deployment in the Far East, I reported to the San Diego Naval Station and Destroyer Base for navy diver's school, where I would take the intensive, one-month scuba course.

The course, as it turned out, was unmitigated living hell. But I took to scuba diving immediately. I loved being underwater. Diving down into its all-embracing serenity was the first time my mind had ever become concentrated and relaxed. Weightless, I was free from the cares of the world.

A few days after graduation I stepped off a military airlift plane at Clark Air Base in the Philippines, proudly wearing my new diver's insignia on my right arm. What with the silver dolphins, the bright red crow of a third-class machinist's mate, the ship's patch that said USS *Rock*, and now the diving hard hat with the letters SD ("scuba diver") inside, I felt like I might finally have an identity on my own, without needing alcohol. I was ready for a fresh start. I jumped on a bus heading to the naval base at Subic Bay, and by late afternoon found my old submarine nestled next to a dilapidated wooden pier. When I reported in to Commander Zekan he seemed pleased to see me.

"How'd you do at navy diver's school?" he asked.

"Oh, not bad," I proudly replied. "I graduated first in the class!"

During the first leg of our deployment, we hip-hopped all over Southeast Asia: Japan, Thailand, Taiwan, and the Philippines. I dove amid deadly poisonous snakes in Okinawa to cut rope off our props, recovered a .45 pistol in ninety feet of silt off of San Fernando, and in practice war games, chased after all the ship's expended torpedoes.

At sea I was a fish; ashore my thirst was so great I wanted to drink the oceans. I had been totally wrong about all of my shiny new achievements doing anything to stop the drinking. It didn't help that I wasn't the only one: everyone, it seemed, was living out my philosophy of getting drunk and being somebody. When I would get back to the boat just before curfew, I'd always find the galley full of drunken sailors, all flopping around like fish out of water. Crewmen torn up on booze often wreaked havoc in the little towns we anchored by: I remember one who ripped the curtains off all the windows in a local club and lit them on fire in the middle of the dance floor. I myself had an incident in which I set off a bag of firecrackers in a bar. Of course, it wasn't long before I got into trouble again.

It was a glorious Sunday morning in Negros, Philippines, when my usual partner-in-crime, Frank Messerli, and I went ashore to get drunk and have some fun. The village next to the dock wasn't much: broken-down shanties, muddy streets, lush foliage everywhere. We found the bars, though, and drank gallons of beer and whiskey. We also scored some "beans," little white Benzedrine tabs that came in a pack like Rolaids. The beans kept us from crashing, so we ended up drinking all day and deep into the night.

It was just an hour before sunrise by the time Frank and I were through carousing, so we staggered back to the dock to catch the launch. Our sub was anchored about half a mile from the shore; the Royal Philippine Navy had provided launch service, using an admiral's gig that came with a crew of two: a coxswain to steer and give signals with the bell, and an engineer to run the little diesel, answering those bells. When we got there, however, the crew was nowhere to be found. I eyed the little boat quietly bobbing there, just beckoning for someone to take it for a ride.

"Come on, Frank. Let's take the admiral's launch!" I drunkenly suggested.

"No, we better not," replied Frank, his head wobbling around.

"Come on, we can do it! You operate the bell and rudder, and I'll get the engine rolling!" We piled in and within seconds had the engine fired up. Then we released the lines, put it in reverse, and started backing out of town. A hundred feet out we turned, switched gears, and poured on the coal. The little engine wasn't running that great—the exhaust emitted

IN TROUBLE DEEP: MY TIME IN THE NAVY | 43

a large cloud of black—and Frank kept passing out with his arm over the helm and his head on his chest, but I kept waking him up by yelling at him, and soon the sub loomed ahead. We could see the topside watch running frantically around on deck, and pretty soon the whole duty section was up waving at us to surrender and come alongside. Running a huge circle, we buzzed the boat at full speed. I could see the captain on the bridge, staring at us through his binoculars. "Well, maybe we better keep going," I thought. We ran a few more circles, smiling and waving to everybody as they ran from one end of the boat to the other. When we finished our loops, we headed for the open sea.

Frank was passed out again, so I took over the helm. I wasn't sure what the plan was, though. In the midst of trying to figure things out, I noticed two small dots on the horizon that seemed to be growing larger. It wasn't long before I realized these were Philippine patrol craft, rapidly approaching. I snapped Frank out of it.

"Frank, let's head for shore. Two patrol boats are chasing us!" We cranked up full throttle and aimed for the beach, hoping to reach shallow water before the boats got to us. Our strategy worked, but we ran aground in the mud, so while I managed the engine and controls, Frank waded around in the muck and finally pushed us free. About this time, I figured we'd best cut our losses and return the launch to where we'd found it. We gingerly followed the shoreline toward town, while the two patrol craft shadowed from deeper water, a few hundred yards away.

As town loomed closer, I saw that half the crew—everyone who had spent the night partying—was on the pier, waiting for their ride out to the sub. As we approached, I could make out the executive officer, and boy did he look pissed. I told Frank that this was our last chance to do something really right, and that we had to make a perfect landing. Frank didn't have a full grip on his duties as coxswain, so I told him when and where to hit the bell. There was only going to be one chance at this landing, so it had to be right. We approached the pier at full speed and aimed for the little boat dock. There were forty American sailors on the dock and a few Filipino officials. Every eye was glued to us as we roared in, pushing a huge, rolling bow wave and leading a trail of heavy black smoke. I waited until I could see the grain on the pilings before I yelled to Frank to ring out three bells. Frank's head rolled around before he came to and rang the bells. I cut the throttle, slapped her into reverse, and then crammed the throttle open as far as it would go.

In the midst of all this excitement, my hat blew off into the water. The boat shuddered and shook as we came smoking in, a mere six inches from the dock. In a sea of froth and black smoke, the little launch came to a perfect stop. We secured the engine and tied her up, while from atop the pier, the crowd let out an earsplitting roar of cheer and applause. Even the Filipinos joined in.

"Well, Testu. Looks like you've lost your hat again," said the old man the next day in the wardroom.

"Yes, sir."

"Tell you what, I'll give you a choice. You can either voluntarily stay aboard the vessel for the next sixty days, or we can have a real Captain's Mast and you'll be busted for sure. What's it going to be?"

I replied, "I'll take the sixty days, sir." I was a "liberty risk" once more.

Next port was Yokosuka, Japan. I got permission from the chief of the boat to go shopping on the base. I then ran to the base chapel for my first confession in a long, long time. An old Irish priest opened the little door. "Bless me, Father," I muttered, "for I have sinned." Then I rattled off the list of my sins as fast as humanly possible, broadly covering each category, making sure not to include any details. "I am sorry for all my sins."

There was a long silence, followed by a deep sigh. "Me boy," the old Irish priest said, "you're headin' for the shoals." He then sentenced me to several Hail Marys and Our Fathers, which I said right there in the chapel, and then, filled with the light of everlasting grace, I returned to the boat and into the sea.

3. HIPPIE DAZE

In 1967 the USS *Rock* was ordered to Vietnam, and we were outfitted with a host of weaponry: two .50-caliber Browning machine guns and an arsenal of small arms, including grenade launchers, Thompson submachine guns, semiautomatic rifles, and .45-caliber pistols. The navy didn't tell us what we'd be doing with all this stuff, but we figured we better learn how to use them. I shot innumerable weather balloons and sunk countless five-gallon coffee tins, never truly thinking about the fact that the real purpose behind this was to learn to kill living beings.

As it turned out, I never had to kill anybody. The war ended, and eventually, my own enlistment reached its end as well. By that time I'd been through three captains, made three WesPac trips, and had been on the boat longer than anyone else. I decided it was time to leave the navy and see what was going on in the rest of the world. After receiving an honorable discharge and a pocketful of freshly printed government cash, I headed up the I-5 corridor for Seattle.

I rented an apartment in a seedy neighborhood of Seattle with two old drinking buddies from high school who had also just left the military. Both worked as traveling TV repairmen. On their daily house calls, they'd hook up this big official-looking meter that read "GOOD," "FAIR," and "BAD"—the "BAD" being in the red zone. No matter what little problem these poor customers may have had, Jon and Ron made the little gadget read "BAD" and would try to sell the victim a new picture tube for several hundred dollars. Then they'd try add on an expensive service contract on top of that. The boys made good money, and I had sufficient funds, so we split the rent and lived on the cheap.

Vaguely hoping to someday become an oceanographer, I enrolled at the local community college. I also was lucky to find a full-time job with the Union Pacific Railroad, working graveyard shift as a roundhouse machinist, who is responsible for making temporary repairs to keep trains running during their journeys. There wasn't much to do at night; my main job was to get the four-engine train to Portland ready to go in the opposite direction. It took me only an hour to switch all the controls and run the four-piece monster up and down the track a few times to test it. The rest of the time I hid out in an old switch engine and slept off what was rapidly becoming a constant hangover.

This was the beginning of a very confused and dark period for me that would last until I met my teacher. When the other university students gathered in the cafeteria to chat, I hit a tavern on Highway 99 to drink. My roommates and I were constantly getting "wiped slick" on beer, cheap wine, and marijuana, doing stupid things like feeding our cat dope or shooting the spear guns from my scuba suit into the plasterboard walls of our apartment.

Eventually our demented world came tumbling down. I was already on probation at the railroad for missing work. One night when my boss caught me sleeping in an idling train he fired me on the spot. Shortly afterward I dropped out of school. Then the landlord came over one day, saw the spear holes in the wall and the horrid squalor we were living in, and threw us out of the apartment.

I packed everything I owned into my mini-bus and headed for California, where I hooked up with some old buddies who were also fresh out of the submarine service. I got a job working for the National Steel Shipbuilding Company as a journeyman pipe tester. After work, I'd head out to my old San Diego drinking haunts. Every night, I drank until the bars closed, then slept in my van.

One night, while drinking at the Red Garter—we affectionately called it the "Gutter"—my life changed irreversibly. I had my usual glow on from drinking tall double screwdrivers, when one of the local submarine groupies, Patty, gave me some LSD. It was the summer of 1969, and the stuff was everywhere. I wasn't really sure what it was, but I had a reputation for being willing to try anything, so I chased one down with a beer and promptly forgot all about it. Patty had actually given me two tabs; one tab was supposed to be for another shipmate of mine, Torpedoman Johnson. But Johnson didn't show up in the next ten minutes, and the pill I'd taken didn't seem to be doing anything, so I popped the other one down the hatch as well and went back to my pool game. Twenty minutes later the pool table started to warp and buckle, and the balls started changing sizes. As the drugs took hold, I began getting physical rushes of pleasure—it felt fantastic just to be alive. I was like a god, and this was heaven on earth. Even the simplest of things took on the deepest significance.

The next morning, I was back to my old, familiar self, but with one important difference: I had lost my fear of drugs. And I was ready for more.

In my search for more ways to get high I met this strange cat named Stevie Greevie, a musician who'd played guitar with Iron Butterfly when they were just a garage band. Later he played with the Wailers out of Seattle. When I met him, Stevie had just gone on a nineteen-day speed trip and had lost sixty pounds. The police arrested him when they found him, all buzzed out, trying to lift a house. Stevie still had needle tracks all over his body, but he said he was off the heavy stuff. Regardless, the people who Stevie hung out with were like animals, huddled in shabby little apartments and blowing their brains out with crank, heroin, rez (a highly toxic paint that people huffed), and anything they could get their hands on. He often rummaged through garbage cans behind drugstores, looking for pills—he didn't even know what they were—which he'd gobble by the handful in hopes of getting high.

Hanging with Stevie, my descent into full-on drug addiction began. Down and down I spun, merging with the dark side. I never did shoot up, but I ate mescaline, peyote, LSD, cocaine, speed, uppers, downers, codeine, grass, and just about anything else I could cram down my throat or stick up my nose. I liked being fried. It made me forget about myself.

Stevie and I moved back to Seattle, where I rented a run-down apartment. I told Stevie he could stay there as long as he didn't shoot up with a needle. We applied for food stamps and lived on rice, butter, and soy sauce. At night, we'd go down into the darkest, slimiest holes to get drunk. Eventually we ran out of money and food stamps, but not before I had driven out to my parents' house in the South End to raid their freezer and "borrow" my little sister's guitar so Stevie could have something to play.

One day I returned to the apartment to find Stevie bouncing off the walls. He had a tourniquet around his arm and was trying to shoot up some hard drugs. He was already very stoned and begging me to help him shoot more, saying that if I were really his friend, I would do it.

I came to my senses. I moved out.

A few months previously I had seen my cousin Mike, one of the only relatives from my "straight" family that had gone hip, at a Doors concert, where he had told me about a country commune set up near Mount Rainier. Before even seeing the place, I decided that I was going to move there. I packed up my cats (I'd somehow collected two pure-bred Siamese) and headed for the commune, called the "Family Farm." It was the winter of 1969, a blanket of fresh snow had just fallen, and the evergreen-laden countryside emanated peace and joy. As I drew closer to Mount Rainier, I felt like I was leaving my past behind.

In the heart of logging country, near a little town called Elbe, I turned off the main highway and drove a couple miles down a narrow country road, slipping and sliding all the way. I found the right driveway, a long two-rut road, and followed it past a couple of small farmhouses, each covered with snow and radiating soft yellow light from their windows into the darkness. I stopped at a wooden gate, let myself in, and drove a half-mile to the main farmhouse, a two-story structure that sat on the top of a hillside. A tall slender man with hair down to his shoulders—he looked somewhat like Jesus Christ—stepped out to greet me. "My name is Dane," he said.

"Hi, I'm Tim," I said. "My cousin Mike sent me."

"Far out," said Dane. He gave me a hug and added, "You are welcome here, brother. You can sleep in Mark's cabin. He's gone back to school." Dane led me across a snowy field to a small shack nestled under a stand of old-growth cedar. We went in and lit some candles. There was nothing in the room but a couple of apple crates and a mattress on the floor. I rolled out my bedding and brought the cats in. After inspecting everything, they settled at the foot of my bag, and we all went to sleep.

The next morning I woke to the sound of chomping. Opening my eyes, I looked out the window to see a horse munching grass just outside the window, about five feet from my face. His breath steamed as he kicked up snow.

I hadn't felt this good in a long time. I got dressed, headed down to the farmhouse, and walked into the communal kitchen, where about ten "family farmers" were gathered around a large homemade table.

"Welcome, brother," one said. They were eating oatmeal and invited me to join in. They introduced themselves: Terry and Skydria; Dan and Marion; Yendor ("Rodney" backward) and Susan (who appeared to be naked); Steve and Susie; Donna and Chuck; and Nancy, Kelly, and Tara. They explained that there were eighteen members of the family, but some were out wandering. As we were talking, my cat Ringo pushed open the door and made himself at home under the stove.

The Family Farm was one of the first anarchistic hippie communes in Washington. The place was a forty-seven-acre property that included a two-story farmhouse, a barn, a chicken coop, a large garden, and several smaller homemade outbuildings. We rented it for fifty dollars a month.

The only rule was that there were no rules. Well, perhaps there was one rule: you couldn't lay trips on anybody.

No one at the commune worked. I was the only one with income, still drawing unemployment from California. The rest lived on food stamps and whatever they could scavenge from dumpsters on the weekly excursions to town. Most of the core group had come to the Northwest wanting to live in harmony with nature after being part of the Haight-Ashbury scene in San Francisco.

Those of us at the Family Farm were convinced we were living proof of the universal brotherhood of man. Everyone met with hugs. Life at the farm was a time for open feelings, a time for sharing, a time for simply being, and a time for public baths. Dropping out was a chance to live naturally and simply in the present—and to ingest as much mescaline, peyote, psilocybin, opium, hash, and grass as possible.

If the ordinary pleasures we'd taken for granted during our straight lives now seemed exciting and wonderful, it was probably because life on the commune was one constant, terrific high. We all liked being stoned, and our goal was to be stoned as much as possible. Personally, I added a balanced supplement of speed and alcohol to the usual psychedelics, so that most of the time, I was neither up nor down, but somewhere in the middle. On special occasions, the family would have a house drop, where everyone took the same drug at the same time.

In the evenings, after family dinner, we'd all go into the living room, get a crackling fire roaring in the woodstove, and become a jug band. Terry would rattle on pots and pans and chant whatever happened to pass through his mind. Dan would cut in with rockin' electric guitar riffs, and the rest of us would join in with sticks, harps, flutes, acoustic guitars, and an old washtub base. The whole house would be cooking all night; we could run a single song for hours.

Since this was the sixties, there were no fixed rules with regards to sex, but most of the folks had coupled up. During the daytime we stayed outdoors a lot, and several of the members, both male and female, felt inclined to walk around naked. Although I was too inhibited to do so myself, I didn't mind the others doing it. And even though I kept my clothes on, I soon shacked up with one of the girls, Kelly, who called herself Dancer. It was fun having someone to snuggle up with in the night, and we shared a common love for cheap red mountain wine.

It was also at the Family Farm that I met the person who would be directly responsible for bringing me to Buddhism. One night, about a month after I'd moved to the farm, we were all sitting around the kitchen table when in walked this guy with red hair to his shoulders, a big red beard, and a beatific face. Everyone rose to greet him with bear hugs, then introduced him to me as Red Al. I felt like I'd run into a long-lost sibling.

Alan had lived in Berkeley during the heyday of the sixties revolution, and had just hitchhiked all the way to the Woodstock festival and back. He lived in an Indian tepee in a remote, heavily wooded section of the farm. Religious by nature, Alan's tepee was filled with books about mysticism, Buddhism, woodworking, and boats (Alan dreamed of one day building his own sailboat). He and I soon became close friends. He was a welcome and positive influence—perhaps the *only* positive influence—in my confused and scattered life.

Alan gave me *The Tibetan Book of the Great Liberation*, and I straightaway became fascinated with Buddhism. I read about yogis who had accomplished incredible states of liberation and enlightenment. I was thrilled by the idea that such a thing was possible in this lifetime, and that perhaps I wouldn't have to wait until heaven for my eternal reward. I started collecting Buddhist books, and carried one with me wherever I went. For a little while, I was content.

I've always thought that the Buddhist truth of impermanence, which I came across for the first time in my reading at the Family Farm, is not so much religion as it is simple common sense: everything in life is of the nature to one day pass away. My blessed time on the farm was no exception; it didn't last, and not even for long.

By the spring of 1970, word of our commune had spread, and truckloads of hippies from Seattle would show up unannounced, bearing offerings of drugs and booze. I had an old klaxon, a diving alarm I'd brought home as a souvenir from the submarine service, which I hooked up on the kitchen porch. Anytime there was a "joint session," or when other drugs were dispersed, someone would sound the alarm, and like cockroaches from a wall, hippies would come rushing in from their rooms and cabins to get stoned with the family. What with all the visitors, the alarm started to ring often—too often—and I began to feel like we were overdoing it. I still had all my marbles, but not everyone could handle the constant onslaught of chemicals. One girl stood out in the woods one night and screamed for hours as if she were being murdered. And for a couple of weeks, Donna, Chuck's girlfriend, ran around naked—which was all right—but muttering to herself and drinking water out of mud puddles.

One summer evening, while flush with drugs and visitors, we threw a yard party. We held a house drop of psilocybin, everyone sitting in the living room and receiving his or her dose like Holy Communion. Before long I saw green rivers of light racing through the passageways of the house. Someone else said they could see them, too. As the sun went down in a shower of red and orange light, the drugs really took hold, and the group hallucination started to get out of hand. To the ghosts and gods and spirits of the area, we thought, our old farm on the top of the hill must have looked like a haunted house in a horror movie, rocking, breathing, vibrating as if alive. We decided that we needed to sate the house's demons.

We dug a huge pit in the front lawn and held an impromptu ceremony, offering to appease the wild and angry spirits of the house. Our goats and dogs and cats stared into the hole, probably wondering what in the hell we were going to do next. Terry dragged our old TV set out of the house and into the yard, where everyone smashed it with a sledgehammer. Then we pushed it into the pit. Chuck stepped to the edge, poured a gallon of gasoline on the twisted mess, and tossed in a match. But the gas had already spilled on the side of the pit and on his pants, and so he caught fire, too. Consumed in flames, he screamed and ran. A bunch of us chased him around the farmhouse, eventually tackled him, and smothered the flames with our bodies.

After this incident Alan and I both agreed that the partying was getting out of hand and that there should be some rules for behavior, especially for limiting visitors and cutting down on the partying. We brought it up to the others, but they would have no part of it. I decided that I needed some space. Using lumber salvaged from abandoned buildings, I built a cabin in the woods, about a quarter mile from the big house, where the wild parties continued.

The all-night, drug-fueled shenanigans began to stir up a lot of hate and resentment in the area. The Family Farm was in the middle of old-school logging territory, and things were highly polarized between the loggers and us hippies. On Friday and Saturday nights the loggers would get drunk and often show up at the farm unannounced. We started locking the gate, but that was no problem for them—they just revved up their Power Wagon and blasted right through it. They would always want to fight us, but we usually were able to talk them down by inviting them into our kitchen and sharing some beers. For a while, we were able to avert disaster.

Then, one Sunday afternoon, a caravan of hippies came from Seattle with an offering of hashish. We held a house smoke session and were just getting off when a bunch of husky drunken loggers appeared in the meadow decked out in typical logging attire: black-and-white striped shirts, high-water Frisco jeans with red suspenders, and steel-toed boon-dockers. It was obvious to all they were here for one reason only: they wanted to kick the living shit out of us.

Normally we'd have tried to do what we always did—soothe them with love (and a little beer) and send them on their way—but at the time we had a rambunctious, hot-headed visitor, who picked up a four-by-four timber and swung it at one of the loggers. When I arrived on the scene, the loggers and hippies were standing off in the backyard, and it looked like all hell was about to break loose.

I ran up to a room on the second floor and grabbed my shotgun, a long-barreled classic that held a single .12-gauge shell. I poked my nose out the little window overlooking the backyard, my heart racing furiously. I planned to chase the loggers away by shooting into the air, but already I could imagine the ramifications of that: they'd come back armed to the gills and kill us all.

Our friend with the board took another swipe at the loggers, infuriating them. I popped a shell into the long chamber and cocked the hammer. The biggest logger, who resembled a bighorn elk, smashed his fist into his hand. "Let's get 'em!" he yelled. My finger squeezed in on the trigger—the fight was about to start.

Suddenly Red Al arrived on the scene.

"Everyone sit down!" Alan ordered in a calm, clear voice. All the hippies immediately sat down on the grass, the women with arms around their children, the men with their legs crossed. The loggers approached the seated group and halted.

"Let's get 'em!" the big moose repeated. Deeply moved by Alan's display of courage, I laid down my rifle, ran downstairs, and sat with the group. Alan, half the size of the largest logger, walked up and talked to the brutes face to face.

"Back off!" one guy warned, but Alan was fearless. The sight of him facing this 250-pound giant with ham-handed fists was unforgettable. Alan talked to him like he was a dear little boy, telling him he shouldn't be out here causing trouble, and that we were all just peace-loving souls. I remember thinking to myself, "This must have been what it was like when Jesus Christ was on earth."

"Let's get 'em," the guy yelled again.

"You can't hit people who are sitting down," someone else said nervously. The loggers seemed confused by the sitting down business. They began arguing among themselves. A medium-size guy took a swipe at the big one, and within seconds the whole gang was fighting each other.

"Back off!" their leader yelled, and when his friends didn't heed his call he smashed them with his massive fists. The sound of bruising flesh, bone upon bone, and violent screams filled the valley as the loggers battled among themselves, ripping their clothes and spilling blood all over the yard. The hippies observed in a stoned stupor, untouched.

"We're making fools of ourselves!" a logger finally shouted. "Let's get out of here!" All of a sudden, like a herd of frightened deer, they hightailed it out of the yard and across the meadow. When they reached our barbed wire fence, rather than walk around to the gate, they scrambled over, ripping their clothes and spilling blood on the barbs. Screaming and yelling all the way, they disappeared out of sight. We hippies stood up—crying, rejoicing, and hugging each other in a big circle.

We may have won a battle, but the war wasn't over. The commune was getting more and more out of control, and I felt helpless to do anything about it. The drugs were making me paranoid, scattered, and confused, and I could never seem to get the right balance of alcohol and drugs in my system to make me feel the way I wanted to. Plus, having no rules meant that too many things weren't right. I was building resentment over the workload especially. I used my unemployment money to buy food for the family and did my share of communal work, but there were some who never contributed anything. It wasn't fair. And I just couldn't shake the feeling that there was disaster on the horizon.

On the night of the August full moon, Dancer and I were sleeping in the cabin I had built in the woods. I had installed a glass pane in the roof, and we were peaceful in the quiet, cool space, the starry sky looking down on us through the window, when we heard screams in the distance. I got dressed, ran toward the main buildings, and found Yendor's shed next to the big house burning. Sawdust insulation he'd put in his walls had caught fire. Flush with adrenaline, I ran through the farmhouse rousing everyone. We tried to put out the fire, but it was hopeless. The main house, tool house, and barn were all in one cluster, each no more than twenty or thirty feet apart, and the vast flames quickly spanned the gaps. Terry and I ran to the barn, where the horses were going crazy, jumping up on their hind feet. We flung open the door, and they ran off into the night. Flames had leapt to the barn just as the volunteer fire department arrived. By the time they got set up, the fire was out of control, reaching into the sky, licking at the silver moon. After a brief attempt to put it out, the firemen turned off their pumps, and we all stood together and watched the place burn. In the ashes of the fire someone found a Bible, badly burned. It was open to a page that said the Holy Ghost would come down upon wings of fire.

It was obviously time for all of us to go our separate ways. Dancer and I bought a hundred-dollar Rambler station wagon (I honestly didn't know where my mini-bus had disappeared to), packed up our belongings— which included a stack of Buddhist books, a billy goat, and a couple of chickens—and headed out across America. Our plan was to let whatever was going to happen, happen. If that didn't work out, we'd try to find a new commune to live on.

We spent a few months driving south, staying with old friends when we could, before arriving in New Mexico, where we found two members of the Family Farm, Terry and Skydria, squatting on some barren land in the foothills outside of Albuquerque. Terry still looked like Neanderthal man, all muscle, naked most of the time, long-haired, and crazier than a March hare. Skydria looked the same, too—cobalt blue eyes and long dark hair—but in the intervening months had for some reason lost use of her legs, so Terry carried her wherever she had to go.

We set up camp next to Terry and Sky. Living mindlessly outdoors, we shared an open kitchen and an adobe stove, and all our pots and pans hung from branches. Using salvaged boards, I made a bed nailed to three trees for Dancer and me. Our nearest neighbors, a rich dropout couple from Brooklyn, lived in an adobe house about half a mile down the creek. Lara was a weaver and Jeremy a banker's son. They kept horses. At night we sometimes heard Lara screaming as if she were being attacked; once we even heard gunshots. I suggested to Terry we go down and check it out, but he said they were just mainlining heroin, then shooting their pistol into the air, and that she screamed like that all the time.

It was the summer of 1970, and refugees from the Haight-Ashbury scene were freeloading all over the foothills of New Mexico. But these communes were not the show of love and light that they were made out to be; there was a lot of thieving and bad behavior, all within some very unsanitary living conditions. Many of the hippies were growing their own marijuana, and thus had to live next to their plants, in constant fear that some greedy predator would harvest them. All of the communes were having trouble with transient freeloaders, burned-out hulks looking for drugs, sex, and a free meal, who would show up for a few days and cause trouble. Just like Family Farm, eventually most of the communities burned down.

These were strange times, and I must admit, I felt strange. I was filled with many fears and nagging doubts about the whole hippie thing. My folks and relatives were concerned, too. I had no plans—no direction, no future, no job, and my unemployment was running out. I knew at heart that I didn't belong where I was; sometimes I felt like I was wasting my life. But where was I supposed to be? What was I supposed to be doing? I had no idea.

One day, when there was nothing in particular to do—which of course could have been any day—I went into town to get the mail. The temperature was in the high nineties, no rain had fallen in months, and the whole state was arid and dry. I picked up a few letters at the post office, then stopped for beer and tobacco at the market. A huge cloud of dust billowed out from under the truck as I turned off the main highway and started chugging up the winding road on my way back to camp. To my right lay the sheer cliffs of San Cristobal; to my left, the endless plains leading off to the western horizon. It was only in the foothills, the narrow band of light vegetation that ran for hundreds of miles to the north and south, that hippie folks like us lived. The few creeks were enough to support thousands of squatters in makeshift camps, tents, adobe huts. But what desolation!

Working the old rattletrap through the gears, I gained elevation and soon could see, through the wiggling heat waves, the endless flat plains below, with the Grand Canyon splitting them like two pieces in a giant puzzle.

My life seemed an equal puzzle, my brain split in a million cracks. I parked the truck on the bluff overlooking camp. Below I could see the creek winding down the hill, and the little stand of trees that had sprung up around the wet soil. Terry's garden was prospering—he was a gardenholic—but I was no farmer. I'd had enough of this starving hippie stuff. I wasn't happy. My whole life I had been living in fear, unfulfilled, incomplete. And for once even booze and drugs couldn't fill the vast, aching emptiness.

Growing up, I had been an enthusiastic Catholic. I regularly participated in the mass, took the sacraments, went to confession, received Holy Communion—the works. There was much I loved about the Holy Mother Church. I adored the huge Saint James Cathedral in Seattle where our teachers ushered us in for the various holy days of obligation. I loved the tall domed ceilings, the feeling of vast space, the padded cushioning on the kneelers, the mild angst before confession, the magical flight of Holy Communion. I loved genuflecting, signing the cross, and reciting the mass in Latin. I loved the power and glory of the ancient organ at St. James with its sweeping array of brass pipes and tubes. I loved being part of a community of like-minded people, rubbing shoulders, sliding on and off the slick hardwood benches in unison, lifting our hearts up in prayer and song. We spent hours at prayer in those hard pews, and when I was younger it always seemed to help. Amid the outer turmoil of my life, back then I thought I had a personal friend in Jesus Christ. I petitioned Him in my hours of need, and He would, it seemed, give me strength to make it through whatever it was I was trying to make it through.

But my Catholicism had been gradually waning ever since my junior year when I was thrown out of high school. Now, looking out over the camp, I knew that when I used to pray that I had just been talking to myself. And what kind of person was I? Left to my own means, out on the road with nothing to enforce my behavior, I had only sunk deeper and deeper, returning to my Catholic upbringing merely when I didn't know how else to atone for everything I had done. As religion slipped further and further away from me, I had turned to drugs to fill my heart. And then I had begun to flirt with insanity.

If you had asked me at that moment what I wanted from my life, I would have answered, truthfully, that all I wanted was to be with God. But I had no idea how to go about doing that or even what that would look like. So instead I reached into the mail sack and found a letter from Red Al, postmarked San Francisco. My pulse quickened. "My search is over," Alan had written. "I've found my teacher. He is a Chinese Buddhist abbot who is kind of like a cross between Jesus Christ and Confucius, and I've become his disciple."

My hands trembled; my heart pounded. Even before I set the letter down, I knew I was going to San Francisco to see Alan and this new teacher. How did I know this? I couldn't tell you. But when God called Paul to become an apostle, he didn't send out invitations—he knocked him off his horse. Venerable Hsuan Hua came to me like that, a bolt of lightning out of the night. The call was sudden, swift, and unexpected— the conditions unseen. Sometimes we simply awaken to our real purpose. Clouds clear to reveal the sun. After endlessly sinking and bobbing in the sea of human suffering, we catch a glimpse of the other shore. And then our true work begins.

Running down to camp, letter in hand, I found Dancer, washing her hair in a clear pool of the creek. I told her about the letter and my decision to go to San Francisco. I figured she'd be thrilled that I'd found my spiritual path. She wasn't.

Still, the next morning, a teary Dancer dropped me off on the outskirts of Albuquerque, where I could hitch a ride to California. I was on my own again, on the road, running loose in the universe.

4. BITTER PRACTICE, SWEET MIND

I found 125 Waverly Place off a crowded back street of old Chinatown in San Francisco where vendors busily trimmed and sold vegetables in dozens of sidewalk stalls. A brass plaque showed me the entrance to the "Buddhist Lecture Hall." I hurriedly climbed four flights of creaky wooden stairs. As I reached the upper landing I saw two old Chinese men talking. One was dressed in drab peasant clothing, the other in a bright yellow robe covered by a red patchwork cape embroidered with hundreds of golden flowers. Although shorter than I, he appeared huge, with a broad round face like a harvest moon.

"Is Alan Nicholson here?" I blurted out nervously.

"Who's?" the old guy in the robe replied. He looked really ignorant— obviously he didn't know much English. The other Chinese gentleman gave a wide smile, revealing a ghastly mouthful of decayed teeth.

"Alan Nicholson," I said.

"Who's?" the monk asked again.

I felt uneasy. Clearing my throat, I raised my voice and yelled, "Alan Nicholson!"

"Inside!" The monk yelled back, and then both men turned to each other and erupted in laughter. Was this really the place that Alan had wanted me to come to?

I entered the room the old guys indicated. The space was about twenty-five by fifty feet.

Clouds of incense perfumed the air. The ceiling was adorned with intricate wooden carvings of gods, men, animals, and dragons. Six red Chinese lanterns glowed dimly. Up front, inside a colossal glass case, sat three buddha statues in gold leaf, legs in full lotus. Below the statues was a handmade pecan lecture chair and a lavish altar overflowing with fresh fruits, flowers, and golden statuettes. All along the walls hung scrolls of calligraphy and pictures of Chinese sages. Where was I?

Forty people were crowded into this tiny space, all sitting in meditation on miniature stools, elbow-to-elbow facing the wall. A few of the sitters looked Chinese, but most were not. The men dressed in loose clothing and the women wore bright dresses. One young girl wore fresh flowers in her flaxen hair. Some appeared to be monks, with shaved heads and long gray robes. One, a little guy with thick eyebrows and full lips, motioned me to a meditation cushion, where I sat quietly until a bell rang.

"Do you know where I might find Alan Nicholson?" I asked. When he replied in a husky female voice, I realized this was a woman, her head shaved. She pointed to the corner. It was my friend Alan all right, but minus his signature shaggy red hair and beard. He now sported short hair, baggy clothes, and a string of beads. His face appeared younger and more peaceful, as if someone had erased the lines. His eyes were clear.

A monk struck a massive bronze bowl about the size of a medicine ball, the sound spilling across the room in eerie waves. Everyone took places before the altar—women on the left, men on the right—and a ceremony began. I stood in back, where a thin Chinese lady crept up and showed me our place in the text. My eyes wandered, Alan smiled, bells rang, drums beat. A monk thumped on a huge wooden fish. Everyone, including me, made full bows, foreheads to the floor.

After a few minutes, an old man appeared from out of the back room. He was the man from the stairs I'd been yelling at. People were calling him "Shifu," which I later found out meant "teacher" or "father." He now wore silk robes, and he reverently bowed to the buddha figures in the case as everyone discreetly stole looks at him. He then selected thick sticks of sandalwood from a crystal jar and pressed them into a cauldron. Although I did not yet know the words in Chinese, those who did began to sing:

> Fragrant incense now is lit, perfuming the Dharma Realm.
> A vast sea of bodhisattvas breathes it from afar.
> Under these auspicious clouds we now request
> With genuine minds, that all buddhas now appear.
> Homage to the enlightened ones, bodhisattvas, mahasattvas.

The people then chanted a series of long mantras to the rapid, opiate beat of the slender red sticks against the wooden fish:

> Namo Ru Lai Ying Gung Jeng Byan Jr Namo Pu Gwang Fo
> Namo Pu Ming Fo Namo Pu Jing Fo Namo . . .

As I learned later, the chants called on eighty-eight buddhas in a ceremony that included repentance for wrongdoing, vows to reform our lives, a promise to seek the Way, and a supplication that buddhas continue to appear in the world. Everyone formed a loose circle and began to walk around the periphery of the room chanting the Buddha's name. The abbot, assisted by attendants, ascended the Dharma seat and locked down into full lotus, the position Buddhists have meditated in for thousands of years: cross-legged, each foot over the opposite knee.

Once the old man was settled into the chair, everyone bowed and returned to the floor. The flaxen-haired girl approached the altar, lit a stick of incense, held it over her head, and then slowly circled the room three times. Then she too placed the stick in the ancient cauldron, returned to center, bowed three and a half times, and on bended knee, made a formal request for Dharma: "Will the Venerable Master, for the sake of this assembly and all living beings, please turn the wonderful Dharma wheel, so that we may quickly learn how to leave suffering, attain bliss, and end the cycle of birth and death?"

The abbot nodded assent and, when everyone settled into whatever form of sitting they could, began his talk. He spoke in Mandarin, reading from four Buddhist texts, or *sutras*, in relaxed musical tones while a monk captured the talk on tape. After reading for a few minutes, the abbot put down the book and gave us a generous smile, then began his commentary. The ceremony and chanting had already relaxed me, and now that the abbot was speaking I felt like I had traveled backward in time—somewhere long before twentieth-century America. Most in the room stared at him in adoration while others sat quietly with their eyes closed. At different parts of the lecture, the monks and others in the audience who understood Mandarin laughed out loud. I laughed too, although I didn't know what was funny.

When the abbot was done, the monk rewound the tape, put on earphones, and began to translate. The abbot had been talking about the exact problem that had been bothering me my whole life, although I didn't know it had a name until now: the mad mind. He referred to it as *pan-yuan* mind, a mind that brings us suffering because it can never be at rest. It constantly climbs on conditions, grasping and clinging to external things as easily as internal ideas; always scheming, calculating, measuring. He made it clear that there's nothing we need to get rid of more than this crazy, wandering mind.

The next part of the talk was on spiritual penetrations, the psychic powers one obtains from cultivating the Way. These powers include the ability to see past lives, to see into the future, and to read other people's minds. We shouldn't seek these powers in and of themselves, he counseled. They would come automatically as a result of our practice. In fact, a good Buddhist shouldn't be attached to either having them or not having them. True cultivators of the Way don't advertise their powers or charge money to use them, he said. They carefully guard their talents, using them exclusively to benefit living beings.

While the monk translated, I closely observed the abbot sitting in full lotus, his eyes closed, palms in mudra, his lips silently reciting a mantra. I was entranced.

When the abbot resumed in Chinese, I slipped into a daydream, thinking how nice it would be if I could conquer my mad mind and have spiritual penetrations. I reflected back to the time I'd spent aboard my old submarine in the Pacific. I had recently started to have nightmares of giant submarines snaking over mountains, or deep in the sea with water gushing in, the boat sinking into darkness. I often woke from these dreams drenched in sweat.

Wouldn't it be great, I thought, *if I could see inside the ocean and watch submarines racing blindly through the night?* I pictured a fast-attack nuke running at forty knots, banking into a steep turn like a stunt plane. I could see my buddies walking around in the galley, drinking coffee and talking, others reading in their bunks—my images clear as a movie. When I snapped out of my reverie, the abbot had finished his talk and the translator was already speaking.

"When you become an awakened being, a bodhisattva, and obtain spiritual penetrations," the translator was saying, "you can see anywhere in the universe. If you want to look inside the oceans of the world, it's no problem. You can clearly see what your friends are doing. Without leaving your meditation bench, without even getting wet, you can watch all the submarines flying around. You can be outside looking in, or inside looking out. Everything is just as you wish."

I cannot describe how shocked I was when I heard these words. My brain burst in a riot of emotions. Wait a minute! How could he see what I was thinking? I couldn't comprehend how anyone could see thoughts so clearly and report them with such precision. How did he do that? How could *anyone* know what I was thinking? Yet I couldn't come up with any other explanation. It was too exact to be coincidence.

I thought back to the first time I had taken LSD, when I realized that my mind was not confined to my own body. Where did my mind end and the abbot's begin? I looked up, and he was grinning at me, his eyes in a squint. I was still flabbergasted. And yet, somehow, I also felt genuinely touched—loved on the deepest level of my being. This was new territory for me. Overwhelmed, I began to weep with joy.

After the ceremony, I found Alan, and we walked back out onto the balcony where I had entered. I reached for my cigarettes, but he informed me that smoking was not allowed. Here, he said, everyone followed a strict regimen based on what was called the five precepts: no killing, no stealing, no sexual misconduct, no lying, and no intoxicants. The monks obeyed 250 rules, the nuns 348, Alan said. Everyone ate only vegetarian food. Laypeople were monogamous, the monks and nuns celibate. "The idea of holding these precepts is not just to be good," he explained. "It restricts your energy outflows, so that energy normally lost and scattered can be concentrated and conserved." By limiting the interaction of the senses with the "outside" world, the powers of perception associated with each sense naturally become clearer, sharper, and more powerful. This, together with the guidance of a genuine teacher such as the abbot, paves the ground for initial enlightenment.

"Initial enlightenment?" I asked.

"The unspeakable breakthrough where the universe is seen as being just a manifestation of one's own mind," Alan replied serenely. "The precepts are the moral foundation upon which all future practices are built."

"Don't you get tired of all those rules?" I asked.

Alan said he asked the same question when he first arrived. The abbot had replied, "There are so many rules because people don't follow rules."

"So you follow all of this?" Alan told me that in the two months he'd been there, he'd followed the rules, listened carefully to the lectures, done a lot of sitting, and now felt incredibly spiritual all the time. I believed him. After all, we'd been high together on many occasions.

Alan led me to the kitchen, a dirty, narrow room with no windows. We brewed tea and counted cockroaches. Guffaw, an ex-hippie who was now the portly temple cook, farted and laughed as he made bread and heated gross-looking leftovers. Alan warned me not to be fooled by all the traditional trappings of the temple. Beneath the clouds of fragrant smoke, he said, were the most penetrating, radical, spontaneous, and profound teachings available in the world. This was not just idle philosophy or some advanced kind of psychology. The abbot taught from the "inside out." His teachings bore no resemblance to the lightweight new-age theories that were being packaged, peddled, and sold all over America. This was no head/mouth rap—all talk and no walk. Nor was it a bunch of confused, "self-enlightened" acid heads. This was the ultimate expression and realization of human religion. Until now, he said, no one in the West had been qualified to teach this kind of stuff. The abbot, Alan emphasized, was qualified.

After the evening lecture, the women packed up and drove across town to their apartment. We men chanted mantras until ten, then it was lights out. I slept on the floor. The next morning, Alan invited me to sign up for the rest of the summer session.

I was really excited by the prospect but also a little dumbstruck. This was everything I'd dreamed of—and ten times more—but I had to think. I needed time to make a decision.

I spent the next two days walking around Berkeley, absorbing the sun, indulging in beautiful sights, and thinking about what to do with the rest of my life. I couldn't get the Buddhist Lecture Hall out of my mind. Deciding not to rush too quickly into the precept regarding intoxicants, I gorged on gourmet meals, fine wines, rich beer, and nothing but the finest cigarettes. But I knew I couldn't go on living like this any longer. I had no job, no girlfriend, no home, no commitments. I was a free man, but I didn't feel free. My spirit yearned to soar. There were worse things I could do than go to this summer session—I'd already wasted my life on many of them. There was nothing better I could think of. What the hell! I had nothing to lose and everything to gain. I decided to go for it.

I returned to the Buddhist Lecture Hall and signed up for the rest of the summer session, agreeing to pay one hundred dollars a month to cover my food and shelter. I slept that evening with the rest of the laymen on the floor of the buddha hall.

At 3:30 A.M. I awakened to a sharp sound—a monk was walking around the temple banging two hardwood boards together. I rubbed the sleep from my eyes and went to the dingy kitchen behind the three enormous buddha statues at the back of the hall. Alan was already there, boiling water for tea. We went upstairs to the rooftop, where it was chilly, foggy, and dark, with a fresh Pacific breeze blowing in over the hill. We sipped tea together while San Francisco snored. The tea was Tieguanyin, an oolong variety that I would later learn was named after the Chinese goddess of mercy Guanyin, the female embodiment of Avalokiteshvara, the bodhisattva of compassion. It was exactly mercy and compassion that I needed right then: looking out at the jutting city skyline, my stomach full of butterflies, I felt scared and uncertain. I had no idea what I had gotten myself into.

Standing upright next to us on the rooftop were three wooden crates that I assumed had been used to ship the massive gold buddha statues from Asia. I peeked inside one and recoiled with a gasp. There was a person in there—a monk, sitting bolt upright in full lotus. Alan explained that the monks had made vows never to lie down, so they slept sitting up, following the abbot's example, who had been sleeping sitting up most of his life. They were hoping to evolve to the point where they didn't really sleep, but just sat, locked in full lotus all night long, their minds in a state of *samadhi*, or meditative concentration.

This vow never to lie down was the thirteenth of the thirteen *dhutangas*, the bitter practices that the Buddha recommended if you ever wanted to get anywhere as a cultivator. Other practices included everything from sleeping under trees at night to making begging rounds in strict succession (not trying to just go to the houses that had good offerings). Well, I soon learned, the abbot didn't ask his disciples to go door-to-door in America, but he did expect them to implement as many of the bitter practices as possible, so as to experience their fruit: the sweet mind. I didn't know it quite yet, but the abbot operated his temple as if we were still in China during the golden age of Buddhism thirteen hundred years ago. At the Buddhist Lecture Hall in 1970, you might as well have been in the Tang dynasty.

In a moment and all at once, the three American monks stretched their legs and climbed out of their individual boxes. Somewhere across town, Alan told me, the women were getting up and going through the same thing. He showed me Chinese stretching exercises designed to get the blood flowing to the brain so that you would have good meditation. The monks in their flowing robes joined in, and soon the rooftop was filled with strange figures dancing in slow motion. I was one of them and feeling better already.

Before we could meditate, however, we had to perform morning services. It was now 4:00 A.M., and I was utterly awake (it helped that there was no heat in the temple and the windows were open). First we performed an incense offering, replete with bells and drums, and then we recited the *Shurangama Mantra*, which at around ten thousand characters is the longest mantra in the Buddhist canon. It took twenty minutes to chant the whole thing. The *Shurangama Mantra* is powerful—so powerful that it is said it can "melt away deluded thoughts gathered in a thousand eons"— and we not so much chanted it as shouted it out, accompanied by the rapid beating of the fifty-pound wooden fish drum. When we finished, my ears were ringing and the silence was awesome.

By now it was almost 5:00 A.M. and time for sitting meditation. Unlike other Buddhist centers back then, meditation periods at the Buddhist Lecture Hall always lasted for a full hour. I had never meditated before, and after twenty minutes or so, my ankles and back felt like someone was boring in with a drill. I fidgeted. I tried everything I could to pass through the pain. Nothing helped. My brain raged, thought following thought in wild succession like ivy climbing a wall—one branch sprouting another, one thought giving rise to ten more thoughts. I couldn't stop thinking no matter how hard I tried; my mad mind was running amok. It was all I could do to make it, somehow, through two full sits.

Unfortunately for me, there was more sitting to come—a lot more. The rest of the day, and all the days to come during that summer, followed the same schedule: after morning services and meditation, the abbot gave an informal Dharma talk, followed by a Chinese class and lunch. (We had to get lunch over with before twelve because many had vowed not to eat after noon, including the abbot himself, who, I would find out, had only eaten a single meal per day for decades—and some days ate nothing at all.) Then there was a calligraphy lesson, another Dharma talk by the abbot or one of the monks or nuns, sitting meditation, and finally a short break . . . followed by more sitting meditation. At 7:00 P.M., we gathered for evening services and a formal Dharma talk by the abbot, which was open to the public. Following the lecture, the laypeople returned home, the nuns drove off to their apartment, and the rest of us chanted mantras until 10:00 P.M., when it was lights out.

The ascetic lifestyle was hard to adjust to, especially after my years of drinking and drugging, but Alan was a great help. He introduced me to the five American monks (*bhikshus*) and nuns (*bhikshunis*), all of whom had just been ordained in a big ceremony in Taiwan. They'd been with the abbot for over a year, and they ran all the ceremonies, gave Dharma talks in the afternoons, and were all deeply involved in translating the Chinese sutras. I called them the "big monks."

There was Babbling Brook, six foot five, Jewish, named for his great eloquence in lecturing. Babbling Brook had already studied Chinese language and philosophy in college and was extremely full of himself. He could speak at length on any topic, without any preparation, or, for that matter, any knowledge of the subject. His younger brother, Ralph, was also there cultivating, although he hadn't yet ordained. Then there was First Boss, the first American monk to leave home, and Buddha's Helper, both ex-hippies from the Pacific Northwest. Before these two buddies came to the monastery, they had delved so far into psychedelic drugs that at one point they were on the verge of turning each other in to the loony bin. How-ever, thanks to the abbot, they had given up drugs, alcohol, cigarettes, meat, and women, and had become Buddhist monks. Although relatively uneducated, they both took amazingly fast to the Chinese language and were already translating the abbot's spoken Mandarin and working on a written translation of the *Lotus Sutra*, one of Buddhism's most important scriptures. The last two American monastics, both nuns, Tall & Thin and Short & Sweet, were also excellent translators. They spent the bulk of their days under headphones, scrunched up in full lotus, listening to the abbot's tapes and translating via their hands and a pair of red-hot IBM Selectrics.

I was much in awe of these people—even a little frightened of them. I sensed a power struggle among them—it seemed to me that they all wanted to be, as the abbot called it, Number One. They were so far ahead of me in their practice I thought I'd never catch up. They could all sit in full lotus without moving for the full-hour meditations, whereas I was terrified of the pain. When it was 10:00 P.M. and time to go to sleep, I was ready to lie down and stretch those legs. The monastics, on the other hand, never stopped cultivating, or at least trying. Even at night, when they were allowed to sleep, they'd stay up into the wee hours working on translations, all on only one meal a day.

Most of all, though, I envied the monks' and nuns' closeness to the abbot—they were always talking to him, learning about translations and perhaps more arcane knowledge. I wanted to have access to his wisdom, too, but I was too shy to talk to him. Of course, it didn't help that I didn't know a word of Mandarin and that his English was dicey at best. I could have asked one of the monastics to translate for me, but for some reason, I didn't feel like I had the right to. After all, as I had been trained, there was a chain of command; if I understood only one thing, it was the seniority system. The real problem, in retrospect, was that I didn't have any self-esteem. I had been indoctrinated by the navy and the Catholic Church to be in awe of authority, and so I was. Somehow I decided that I could either take my problems to the American monks or just try to solve them myself. I opted for the latter.

It didn't help my inferiority complex that the abbot was like no one I had ever met before. One beautiful summer afternoon, after the noisy rhythm and clatter of ceremonies, when everyone was settling in to hear the lecture, I overheard him quietly turn to Ralph and tell him to keep a particularly close eye on people. He warned him to watch the door "because there was someone present in the building who was here to steal." Ralph seemed to quickly forget what the abbot had said—but I didn't. Maybe I felt the abbot was also talking to me. I had noticed that he had a way of doing that.

When the lecture ended, the place erupted into the usual hubbub of chitchat and socializing. While everyone was enjoying their tête-à-tête, including Ralph, I noticed a middle-aged Asian woman go into the vestibule off the main hall and try to rifle the donation box. It was like a living dream: first the prophecy, then the reality. The abbot's mind seemed to be able to seamlessly flow in and out of the future, and he was taking me along for the ride.

I alerted Ralph, who rushed in and caught the woman in the act. He took the money out of her hands and shooed her out of the temple. The abbot had already gone to his room, but his words echoed in my mind. I hadn't forgotten about the submarine incident my first day at the Hall, but after some time passed I had already written it off as coincidence; how could he have *really* read my mind? That would have been impossible. But now it was happening again: he actually knew what this person was going to do before she did it. I simply couldn't get over it. It seemed to be as natural for the abbot to read her mind, or my mind, or anyone's mind, as it was for me to speak English. How did he do it? Where did he get these powers? What kind of incredible state was he in, anyway? And why was he revealing himself to me? Would I be able to do this kind of stuff if I cultivated? These incidents caused my faith in the abbot, and in Buddhism, to take seed. I really believed in this wonderful teacher—even though I didn't have any idea who he actually was. I became determined to learn more about this amazing person.

5. SHIFU

The abbot was born in rural China in 1918 as An Tzu, the youngest of eight children. When he was eleven, he found a dead child in the bushes. He decided then and there that he wanted to become a monk and learn how to escape the vicious cycle of birth and death. His mother said that he could leave home and ordain, but first he had to stick around and take care of his parents for a while. He obeyed his mother's wish, warming his parents' bed in winter (in Manchuria many beds were set upon a brick fireplace), fanning them in summer, and quickly gaining a reputation throughout the area as being an extremely filial son.

At the age of fifteen he met his first teacher, the Venerable Chang Zhi. He was given the Dharma name To Lun (Turning Wheel) and studied a wide range of subjects, including philosophy, medicine, divination, astrology, and physiognomy. But his favorite studies were the Buddhist sutras, and many of these he memorized completely before teaching them to his fellow villagers, who were illiterate. Under the guidance of Chang Zhi, he also learned how to meditate.

To Lun's mother died by the time he was nineteen. He honored her memory by building a tiny A-frame hut out of sorghum stalks, a type of sturdy grass, next to her grave, where he meditated and studied. He sat there day and night in full lotus, vowing to never lie down. He ate only one meal a day—vegetarian offerings brought to him by local Buddhists—and did not cook for himself. If no offerings came, he didn't eat. Clothed only in a rag robe, he endured the fierce Manchurian weather for three full years, never leaving the graveside. During that time, he studied the great Buddhist sutras: the *Lotus Sutra*, the *Flower Garland Sutra*, the *Shurangama Sutra*, the *Diamond Sutra*, the *Heart Sutra*, and so on. It is said that he obtained enlightenment there at his mother's grave.

When the three years were up, having fulfilled his vow of filial piety, he walked to Three Conditions Monastery in Harbin, the capital city of China's northernmost province, shaved his head, and ordained as a novice monk. He then moved into a cave in the forest. There he practiced fierce asceticism, eating only pine nuts and drinking mountain water, taking his enlightenment even deeper.

Even though the Japanese were occupying China during this period and travel was dangerous, in 1946 To Lun began to wander extensively, going from monastery to monastery, giving Dharma talks everywhere he went and doing his best to support elder monks by working at everything from cleaning pit toilets to sweeping floors. He took full ordination in 1947.

After two years and two thousand miles of travel, in 1948 the young Master To Lun arrived at the monastery of Venerable Master Hsu Yun (Empty Cloud), who at that time was 108 and the living patriarch of the Chan sect, a very famous monk in China. Empty Cloud certified To Lun's enlightenment, and later, formally transmitted the Dharma to him, making him the ninth patriarch of the Weiyang lineage. He also bestowed on him the name Hsuan Hua (Proclaim and Transform). "Thus it is. Thus it is" were the only words exchanged during this transmission.

Eventually, of course, the Communists took over China, appropriating monasteries, desecrating their sacred art, and ending the practice of Buddhism. Some monks and nuns avoided the slaughter by returning to lay life. In 1949 Master Hsuan Hua escaped to Hong Kong, where he established his first monastery, Western Bliss Garden, and aided monastic refugees from mainland China. Later on he started up a little temple on the eleventh floor of an apartment tower in Happy Valley called the Buddhist Lecture Hall. He also took on the formidable task of constructing a monastery on Lantau, one of the remote islands in the Hong Kong archipelago.

In 1962, Venerable Hsuan Hua moved to San Francisco, where he quietly cultivated the Dharma in a little house. Eventually, however, word of his presence began to spread around outside the Chinese immigrant communities. Other Americans began to seek out the master and ask him to instruct them in meditation. Soon afterward the crowds grew, and so the master and his students rented the Buddhist Lecture Hall in Chinatown, San Francisco, which is where I found him. Eventually, his network of organizations would be renamed the Dharma Realm Buddhist Association (DRBA), which is what it's still known as today.

That is what I learned from the DRBA's biography of the abbot. This is what I learned just from being around him that summer:

The abbot taught an incredible number of people. Since I had only limited access to him, I had no idea what his actual scope was. But I gathered that he had tens of thousands of disciples in Hong Kong, Taiwan, and other Buddhist countries in Asia. He dealt with many of them over the phone. And here in the United States, the number of young Americans studying the Dharma was growing rapidly. Many people came and left, though—only a few stayed. I could never tell who was going to stay and who wasn't, although it wasn't much of a mystery why so many people didn't stick around.

The abbot had conducted his whole life with great discipline, and he didn't conduct the Buddhist Lecture Hall any differently. I said earlier that at the Buddhist Lecture Hall in 1970, you might as well have been in the Tang dynasty. Well, that wasn't entirely true; there were some important differences. During the Tang dynasty, for instance, it was common for teachers to physically beat their disciples into enlightenment. Here in America, the abbot said, we were too soft, and Buddhism was too new, so there was no way he could physically beat us (even though he was "sure we needed it," and that undoubtedly it would "do us some good"). Instead, his "beatings" were mental—mind to mind.

Oftentimes the abbot would go off on us all: "All of you people! Nobody knows how to renounce anymore! Every day you waste away. I give you my flesh, my bones, and my blood, and all you do is laugh and play. What's with all this arrogance, obstruction, and jealousy? Where is the boundless bodhisattva mind? What happened to all of your vows? I can't find one person who understands anything! Where is the respect for the ancient ones who cultivated before you? Has all their work been in vain? Why do you spend all day long talking about other people's faults and good points? 'He did this; she did that . . .' You need to renounce yourself and do the Buddha's work. And don't be so self-absorbed!"

So if we students—and as the summer passed, I began to count myself among them—wanted to get enlightened and obtain samadhi, we'd have to toughen up and learn to take the drubbing. The abbot wrote a little verse that addressed this principle, which he repeated to us over and over again:

Everything is a test
To see what you will do
If you don't recognize what's before your face
Then you must start anew

Right at the start of the summer session, the abbot informed us that he would definitely be testing us—it was his obligation as our teacher. He'd be cheating us if he didn't do it, he said. Some of these tests would be very hard to take, and he predicted that most of us would run away, but that was no problem. "Run all you want," he would say. "There's no way out of the universe." When we got tired, he'd be waiting for us—his door was open. He would neither beg us to come in nor ask us to leave.

The abbot had the ability to turn emotions on and off as easily as drawing hot or cold water from a tap. I had never seen anything like it. One minute he'd scold someone at the top of his voice, the next instant he'd sweetly inquire of someone else. His anger, if that's what one could call it, seemed real, yet it also seemed like he had no attachment to it. It was just another hammer in his arsenal of teaching tools. He'd sometimes burst forth with tremendous blasts of power, shaking the windows and rattling the walls, and then relinquish it all the moment it left his lips.

"What are you afraid of?" he would bellow. "To bear suffering is to end suffering!"

And while the abbot certainly didn't make a habit of explaining his unusual techniques, he did once concede that his job was to get us oscillating between opposites—between good and bad, fear and love, happy and sad, inside and out, so on and so forth—until we got to the point where we no longer lurked in the illusions of opposites, the world of dualities, the idea of a separate self in an "outside world." His teachings cut to the quick, but he was always sure to attack our attachments, not our being—our self, but not our self-esteem.

As for me, I figured everything had its price. For material goods and temporal pleasure we fools gladly suffered and toiled our lives away, I realized. Sure, we got the goods, but we didn't get to keep them for long. Then losing them, we suffer. Why toil for naught? Spiritual goods were ours for the taking, if we worked for them. Those who kept an open mind, who patiently practiced, and who acted sincerely would get a response, I was taught, a response exactly commensurate with the practice. The more we paid, the greater the payback—it was spiritual karma, directly proportional and without fail. I'd just have to do like the rest and bear a little pain, use a little patience.

Actually, that summer the abbot was very gentle and kind with me, but he really laid into some of the others, especially the monks and nuns. Of course there were days when we'd all get it, but he devoted his primary scolding energy to the ordained people. The abbot was constantly pointing out their faults, alternating between building them up, nourishing their egos and attachments, and then letting them fall back down, chipping away at their self-absorption.

If nothing else, it was fun to watch. Sometimes he'd pick one tiny little thing they'd done and then blow it all out of proportion. For the next few weeks he'd drag it up again and again to drive his point home, showing us how we were all caught up in the three evils of greed, hatred, and stupidity, and how we could get rid of them by using morality, concentration, and wisdom. He was always encouraging the monastics to cultivate what he called "awesome manner": "Don't walk around with your heads lowered, going 'Mee-mee, moo-moo!'" he would yell at them. "Don't act like a bunch of frogs! Walk tall and proud, be fierce and fearless, and emit blazing light. Wear your monk's robes with pride. Walk like the wind! Sit like a bell! Stand like a pine!"

The abbot often screamed at Babbling Brook in particular. Bhikshu Brook was certainly a mixed bag. He was educated, eloquent, and smart, but there was something about him, some inexplicable quirk that was obstructing his progress with the Dharma. One day, for example, he was chatting on the phone with a laywoman—a young and attractive laywoman. They were discussing the offerings she was planning to bring to the temple. The abbot was always instructing all of the monastics that under no circumstance should they ever scheme, calculate, or take advantage of conditions. This was a very big thing with him. He even wrote a poem explaining these basic principles, which later came to be the motto of the DRBA:

> Starving to death, we don't beg.
> Freezing, we don't scheme.
> Dying of poverty? No problem!
> We renounce ourselves to do the Buddha's work.

We accord with conditions, but don't change.

Our actions reflect our principles.

We carry on the mind-to-mind pulse of the patriarchs.

But Bhikshu Brook had forgotten the motto, and somewhere in the course of his unnecessarily long conversation with the laywoman managed to let her know that bringing an offering of fresh cottage cheese would be a good idea. This, of course, was not the workings of an unmoving mind. It was a mind reaching out over the phone wires, a mind climbing on conditions, a mind of a person grasping, clinging, scheming, and calculating. It was a clever monk taking advantage of a layperson, a cardinal sin in the abbot's book.

The next day, when he entered the hall, he immediately tore into Babbling Brook. He gave him holy hell for getting so sticky with a woman, blasted him for plotting about the cottage cheese, and continued to roast him ceaselessly about it for several months. "You stupid idiot! All you do all day is false thinking, false thinking, false thinking. How am I supposed to teach you? Your self-nature is worse than a stinking, rotten can of worms!"

This isn't to give the impression, however, that the abbot was always fierce. One afternoon that summer, the head monk, First Boss, gave a little Dharma talk. There were only seven of us in attendance, since the big crowds usually came at night when the abbot spoke. First Boss shared with us that he'd been having a lot of problems—worrying about his family, his future, his past, and so on. Finally he couldn't stand it any longer, so he took his heavy burden to the abbot. He said, "Shifu, I this . . ." and "Shifu, I that . . ." and rattled on for about fifteen minutes, unloading all his problems.

The abbot listened patiently, and when First Boss was all done, he asked, "First Boss, would you like some grape juice?" He then walked over to his little cubbyhole in the back of the hall, rummaged around, and produced a quart bottle of Welch's grape juice. The two of them sat there and drank it together. No further words were spoken, and First Boss said he could feel his troubles melting away.

In fact, as much as the abbot blustered and stormed at times, it didn't take me long to realize that he preferred to direct his teachings to the underdogs, the ones struggling to survive. He knew who was sincere and who was not, and who needed his attention. Cries for help were always heard by him. And whatever he was doing and however he was doing it, one thing always remained constant: he gave the buddhas and bodhisattvas credit for everything, and none to himself. "Don't get the wrong impression," he loved to say. "I'm nobody, a big nothing."

In truth, though, the abbot wasn't nothing—not to me or to many other people. He was so much wiser and more compassionate than anyone I'd ever seen. The things he did were so simple, and sometimes even silly, but for some reason they had such an impact on me that I often found myself crying with happiness. I was sure that most people would laugh at such a foolish fascination. But then who were they to know what was going on? The abbot was truly extraordinary.

As the summer progressed, my heart began to center around a single goal: to produce a mind of enlightenment. My life finally felt like it had a sense of direction. If I could just reform my bad habits and clear my mind out, I thought, even such a fool as me might be able to reach liberation.

6. HE WHO TRANSGRESSES

I know what you're thinking: and what about the drinking? Well, somewhere in the shuffle of all my meditation and Buddhist studies that summer I had more or less unconsciously cut off some pretty heavy habit-energy, and I was flying high, in the best sense of the term. I'd been smoking cigarettes for eight years, and I'd dropped that habit at the door of the Buddhist Lecture Hall as well, barely even noticing the nicotine withdrawal. But this didn't mean that I didn't suffer from a couple of slip-ups.

I remember there was one particular day, after weeks of relentless cultivation, that Alan and I bailed out of the hall and took a bus across the bay to Berkeley. There we splurged on a nine-course vegetarian banquet—a feast capped off with forbidden pitchers of gourmet beer and a couple bottles of expensive wine. We caught a live jazz show featuring a mutual friend of ours and indulged in a package of high-quality cigarettes. We knew full well that it was all against the precepts, but we simply couldn't get ourselves to stop. The excess energy pent up from cultivation was just too much for our limited skills to handle, so we felt the need to vent it off. At the time, anyway, it all seemed outrageously funny, and we laughed the night away.

A bit before 10:00 P.M., however, the funds were blown and it was time to return to the hall. Reeking of booze and tobacco, we suddenly felt defiled, dirty, guilty. We walked into the hall and felt sure everyone knew what we'd done. The Great Assembly, which is what we called the community there, was circling around the perimeter of the hall, chanting the Buddha's name with their one, pure mind, and here we were: a pair of filthy, rotten scoundrels!

No one had to say anything.

After that incident I decided it wasn't worth it anymore to mess with the toxins—it was too much out of sync with the pure energy in the hall. So I really did quit—I vowed to totally give up drinking and smoking. The abbot told us that if our minds remained locked by gruesome black qi energy, it would be impossible for us to realize our infinite buddha natures, our potential for awakening. Who wanted to lose spiritual ground?

I did well for the rest of the summer session. But when it finished and I returned to Seattle, moving into a communal house in the northwest part of the city, I found it increasingly difficult to keep the vows I had made to myself regarding intoxicants. I interviewed for a part-time job as a fry cook at one of the big downtown restaurants, grilling massive amounts of steak and burgers, and now and then a fish. It was hard, but I stuck to my vegetarian diet that I had adopted at the Buddhist Lecture Hall. On one side of the restaurant I served a window where go-go girls ordered food for customers at the cocktail bar. They were cute . . . but no, I couldn't let them bother me. I tried to remain as I had been taught by the abbot: "Thus, thus, unmoving."

All my hippie friends were still pursuing free love, smoking dope, and meandering about aimlessly, but I was beginning to rethink the whole "free love" thing. According to the abbot and all orthodox Buddhist literature, sex was an outflow that impedes advanced cultivation. The ancient worthies gave it up completely. After we die, they said, the craving for sex draws us back into the womb and sets us up for another life caught in the net of our own karma. Sex was the root of ignorance. (This teaching, needless to say, was not very popular at that time.)

I stayed in Seattle for a few months, but all I could think about was the abbot, Buddhism, and the enchantment of cultivation. Worldly pursuits now seemed singularly empty and meaningless. Although I still felt somewhat high, my bright light of cultivation and purity I had earned from that extraordinary summer in San Francisco was rapidly diminishing as I slowly went back to my usual ways of living. The world was getting to be all too familiar and ordinary for me—especially now that I knew there were other possibilities. Eventually, inevitably, and ultimately, I decided to return to the monastery.

Flush with the funds I'd earned from slinging meat and fish, I purchased a cherry 1950 Chevrolet Hardtop and used it to float back toward Frisco on a golden cloud. I picked up a couple of hitchhiking women on the way, and together we drank my mother's homemade wine, sang songs, and camped the whole way to California. They bailed out in Sacramento, and I had to spend a day in the Bay Area just sobering up.

When I got to the temple, they were about to start an intensive ninety-eight-day winter meditation session. The American monks, with the abbot's permission, had designed this session in imitation of the famous Chan sessions held in China. It consisted of a twenty-one-hour schedule, starting at three in the morning and ending at midnight. Throughout the day there was nothing but one-hour sits, followed by twenty minutes of fast walking. This was hardcore Chan.

"When it's too tough for everyone else," the abbot liked to say, "it's just right for us!"

The pain a beginner experiences sitting through one hour of meditation is unspeakable. The pain experienced in a full day of this kind of sitting is unimaginable. We, of course, weren't required to sit in full lotus, or even half lotus, but we did have to keep awake and stay still—how else could we develop our spiritual *gongfu*, our power of meditation? The session was so tough that all the American monks dropped out by the end of the first week. (Suddenly it seemed very important to them that they work on their translations and other publications.)

I was on the verge of dropping out myself. Instead of meditating, I spent a good deal of time contemplating various problems and feeling terribly sorry for myself. One day, while I was midway through a miserable sit, the abbot came out from his room behind the buddhas, walked quietly past everyone, stopped in front of me, and began gently stroking my forehead in a circle. It felt as if the light of the sun were pouring from his hand and going through my entire body. My deluded thoughts vanished and my troubles disappeared. He didn't speak a word, but my spirit was healed. And then he was gone, leaving me to finish the sit with tears streaming down my cheeks.

It's all a question of roots, the master told us. The Dharma was the rain. Those with shallow roots couldn't absorb much water. They wouldn't be able to stay long at the monastery because they couldn't see what was truly happening. Those with deep roots, however, would be deeply nourished.

I didn't know what kind of roots I had, but I kept at the practice even though it didn't seem I was accomplishing anything. I'd start out in half lotus and stay there until I couldn't take the pain any longer, then I'd downshift into no lotus, and finally I'd have to swallow my pride and just let my feet stretch out in front of me for a few minutes. I experienced some very interesting states of mind, but by listening to the abbot's lectures I was able to ascertain that in the big scheme of things they were really nothing to get excited about, much less to mention. The important thing, I learned, was to just keep meditating.

I made it to the end of the second week before I dropped out. The temple was too small, I rationalized. There were too many distractions—people going in and out. My energy was building up and I couldn't sit still. I simply wasn't ready for such a heavy undertaking. I quit.

Out the door I went, looking for work. God, it felt great to be out and about, celebrating the glorious day! I found a part-time position working as an orderly in a home for the elderly in southern San Francisco. My job was to take care of a dozen or so old people who were unable to help themselves. It wasn't a pleasant experience—I was moved to nausea many times over the first few days. None of these people knew how to face death, it seemed, but once they entered this home, death was the only way they could escape. It was as if they suffered a mass psychosis, a group illusion. Here they were losing their homes, friends, relatives, possessions, even their bodies and intellects, and yet most of them tried to hang on desperately to everything as long as possible. Seeing them so hopeless and miserable made me feel almost constantly sad.

I was assigned to the second floor where they kept the folks who were quite far gone—a hundred or so, all stuck in wheelchairs. They had long since lost the will to live, their spirits hollow and waning, but through the wonders of modern medicine, they were kept alive in their sad and empty state, often for many years. I and the other aides dressed them, spoon-fed them, and even assisted them in going to the bathroom since they didn't have enough muscle power or the inclination to do it themselves.

One day an old woman came to the home, checked in by her concerned family. I could see that it was very painful for them to commit her. This woman struck me as being very elegant, intelligent, and independent, but because she was slightly absent-minded, she couldn't live on her own. The day after her admission, I was walking down the hall on the second floor when I heard terrible cries coming from the women's bath, a large tiled room with a standalone tub in the middle. Alarmed, I burst in to find the old woman stark-naked, spread-eagle in the tub, with four huge nurses' aides—one on each limb—holding her down. The fifth aide had just administered an enema, and the tub was vile with runny excrement. The aides were in a delirious frenzy, smirking and enjoying their fiendish pleasure. They knew this woman still had some spirit, and they were out to destroy it as quickly as possible. I told them to quit, but there was nothing I could do—it was all over, the damage done. The woman wept in a low drone. The aides rinsed her and dressed her in a white gown and put her to bed. From that day on she was never the same.

What I saw at the old folks' home drove in deeper the lessons I was learning at the temple. The once colorful and appealing outside world had long since paled to gray. Anyway, I'd already seen half of it—I'd steamed all over the Pacific, seen many parts of Asia, driven over most of the USA. What I saw around me now was suffering, impermanence, and people chasing shadows. We were born confused, lived confused, and died confused. We'd been wrongly taught from birth that the body and intellect constituted our entire self, and that was it; everything outside was something else. We spent a lifetime nurturing, developing, and caring for this illusory self. Within this illusion, the intellect moved ceaselessly—categorizing things, labeling, filling in the boxes—so even the slightest hint of an infinite, nondualistic buddha nature was covered. Our original, sage mind was replaced by the common, conditioned mind, a mind caught up in the poisons of greed, fear, anger, and stupidity. And then when it was time to die, we couldn't let go of any of it.

Every evening I listened to the abbot's Dharma talk, and throughout the day I watched over the workings of what I thought was my mind. In myself and others, I observed the motion of the mind of greed—always moving, seldom content, tangling in the senses, seeking, searching, delving into the past and future for objects of desire, firmly establishing the illusion of self and others, of inside and outside. Even when it gets what it wants, this grasping mind is never happy, because then it has to worry about keeping what it has got. It lives everywhere except in the now, recoiling from the present—running, hiding, escaping, or worse, lashing out at the world.

With the abbot, I had found a rare opportunity to transcend the normal boundaries of human experience. I was no longer satisfied with just getting by. It seemed like I had been viewing the world like a frog inside a deep well—looking up at a little circle of sky all his life, convinced that was the extent of the universe, not knowing of the vast empty space out there. Now I had found an experience unavailable to most people, and

I wanted to take advantage of it. I wanted to end the cycle of birth and death. I wanted to be able to enter a state of unending samadhi, to develop spiritual penetrations like the abbot. I wanted to become a person of the Way without a mind—a living dead man, one who has cut off the basis of affliction, who is vitally alive and centered in the Now, stripped of anxieties and attachments, and who has accomplished the shift of identity from the impermanent self to infinite nature. I wanted a heart stretched beyond the limited view of self unto its fullest limitless potential, so that inside and outside fused together to become one. I wanted to see the whole universe as just part of my original mind. I wanted to break through the ugly barrel of black qi, burst out of the gloomy mass of conditioned thinking wrapped around my brain. I wanted to live the lives of the cultivators I had read about: I wanted to open enlightenment, spend a lifetime helping others on the path to awakening, then eventually forecast my own death and die without sickness or pain, sitting in the full lotus position.

One day, just to start the ball rolling, I informed the head monk that I wanted to take the five precepts—not to kill, steal, lie, engage in sexual misconduct, or ingest intoxicants of any kind—and to take refuge with the abbot, officially converting to Buddhism and declaring the abbot my teacher, which would involve moving into the Buddhist Lecture Hall. A couple of days later the abbot approached me to let me know that there was going to be a refuge ceremony in a few minutes. He asked me if I really wanted to do it. I told him I was sure. He smiled and returned to his tiny room in the back. The ceremony was about to begin when one of the American monks rushed out and told me that if I wanted to take refuge I'd have to shave my beard.

Now, I had grown quite attached to my beard in the short time I'd had it. It made me seem really rough and masculine, very Northwesty. Dark and curly, it was part of my chosen identity. Suddenly I was being forced to make a choice. What was more important: some scruffy facial hair, or taking refuge with the everlasting triple jewel of the Buddha, Dharma, and Sangha? I ran into the bathroom and shaved off my beard. I even gave my hair a bit of a trim. When I came out the ceremony was already up and running.

A couple of other Americans also took refuge. The abbot, using some method known only by himself, gave us names from a choice of about fifty thousand Chinese characters. It was uncanny, the way the names applied to the people that received them. For example, one of the disciples was given the name Kuo Li. He didn't know what it meant, but after the ceremony he gave the master a present of lapis lazuli, a stone he had kept in his private collection for many years. No one knew he had it, or that he was going to give it. Later, when he looked up his name in the Chinese dictionary, he found that it meant "lapis lazuli"! I was given the name Kuo Yu (he who transgresses, or goes beyond the limit). I loved my new name and was very proud of it, for I had gone beyond the limits all my life and didn't plan on stopping now.

After the ceremony a bunch of Cantonese ladies were milling around the hall. The master came out, and they all flocked around him like iron filings to a magnet. He looked at me and started laughing.

"Look at this stupid Westerner!" he said. "He just shaved off his nice beard so he could take refuge with me. Ha!"

My face stung with embarrassment, but there was nothing I could do to bring back the beard. I sulked over to a meditation pad to hide my feelings. I'm sure I actually felt a chunk of my ego fall off and hit the floor. My identity was going south, and there was nothing to take its place. My journey on the Buddhist path had officially begun.

7. GOLD MOUNTAIN MONASTERY

Although a few ran away, most of us survived winter in the cramped quarters of the Buddhist Lecture Hall. In the spring the master informed us we'd be moving to a new home in the Mission district. He'd just bought a huge three-story building, and we were going to transform it into a monastery. We'd call it Gold Mountain Monastery, in memory of the famous training temple in China, and because the Chinese refer to San Francisco as "Old Gold Mountain."

When I heard the news I was in the first wave out to see the place. What excitement! I pictured a romantic setting—perhaps in the style of the early California missions—with stucco walls, open courtyards, grape arbors: the works. This was really going to be something. What I found, however, was a dilapidated old brick structure that had last been used as a mattress factory.

Our new "monastery" was located smack-dab in the heart of the ghetto at the corner of 15th and Albion, directly across from a low-income housing project, a sprawling cement complex—an open-door jail of sorts—that housed the city's poor and a good portion of its criminals. Abandoned hulks of Cadillacs, Lincolns, and Oldsmobiles adorned the streets. Filthy piles of wine bottles and old newspapers littered the sidewalks. Nearby, pushers, pimps, and prostitutes lurked behind the dark corners of graffiti-covered walls. We'd soon find that most any night one could hear screaming, sirens, and now and then, a murder.

The previous owners had removed all the mattress-making equipment, leaving behind a totally vacant building. Actually, it was two buildings, an older and a newer, built side by side and sharing a common brick wall in the middle. From the outside it looked like only one. Other than a depressing knotty-pine office on the first floor, there were no rooms or partitions, just six giant empty floors. The master's plan was to use the bottom-left floor as the buddha hall, and the bottom-right area as the kitchen and dining area. Second-floor left would be the library and visitor reception center; second-right would be partitioned off and fashioned into several dorm rooms and a bathroom for the women. Top-floor left would be men's dorms, and top-right a bathroom and a few more men's rooms. The upper-right corner was reserved for the abbot's quarters and would include an outer reception room. We would do all the construction ourselves.

I continued working at the old-folks' home part-time and tried to be an ascetic full-time. I moved from Chinatown to the top floor of Gold Mountain with the rest of the boys, all of whom zealously slept sitting up in their shipping crates. One of the texts in the Buddhist canon states that there are four stages of sleeping sitting up, the ultimate being full lotus without any support. A lesser stage uses one point of back support, and at the bottom of the list they mention something about having four places of support.

I decided to give this practice a try. I constructed a special box from scrapwood, with armrests and comfortable padding. My unit, with its sloping backrest and generous arm supports, definitely fell into Category Four. But with plenty of blankets and extra pillows, I was somehow able to get through the night in a more or less vertical position. I didn't get much rest, however, because the guy next to me, Bruce Mengbean, an aspiring monk-to-be from Yale, cried out in his sleep—specifically, lines from *Macbeth*. (I thought it ironic that the master had already named him Kuo Meng, "the Dreamer.")

There were a lot of cultivators with Ivy League backgrounds around then, and though Shifu was doing his best to help me toward enlightenment, all that had awakened thus far were my competitive instincts. I came into my own during the remodel work, because we were doing physical labor, but the Ivy League guys were out of their element. I worked a lot with a Harvard grad who would actually go on to become a well-known Buddhist studies professor. I would be hammering up a storm, but the scholar, with his thick glasses and academic demeanor, was struggling with each nail. When the master came by and saw the two of us working side by side, he would burst into laughter.

The construction continued, and I moved on to working by myself on the second floor below the abbot's quarters, doing the job just like a real carpenter might, except that I split my two-by-fours in half, making them two-by-twos. I doubt that the codes allowed it, but this saved money and got the job done just as well. It was Shifu's idea, actually.

One afternoon, while building a new twenty-foot partition, I realized that I'd measured wrong in one spot. It really wasn't much; I was off by only half an inch. I'd already invested several hours in the wall and didn't feel like tearing it down and starting over. I climbed my ladder, looked at the wall from several angles, and decided there was no way the bad measurement would affect the room. Furthermore, there was no way anyone would ever notice it. So I covered my mistake and continued on.

About that time, however, the master appeared. He walked directly to the spot where I had measured wrong.

"Are you sure that board is in the right place?" he asked, pointing to the exact area I had mismeasured. I almost fell off the ladder.

"Yes, Shifu," I automatically lied, my face flushing. There was no way anyone could have possibly known what I had done unless they'd seen me do it; I'd been the only one in the room.

"Don't you think it might be off just a bit?" the master asked as he walked around the perimeter of the room. Good Lord! He had to have been inside my mind to know this.

"Uh, maybe I better check it again, Shifu," I said. The master smiled, looked me directly in the eyes, then left the room, leaving me once again a basket case of twisted emotions. One gets that way when the mind is stripped naked.

That evening during the sutra lecture I felt the master speaking directly to me, heart to heart. His energy warm and clear, he spoke gently and compassionately through my false coverings, and I opened to him.

"While cultivating the Way," he said, "if you're off by an inch in the beginning, you're off a thousand miles in the end."

I understood.

Throughout the construction, we continued to work on our Chan sitting, balancing hard work and meditation. The early morning sits were best. I especially remember the cold and foggy air, blown in fresh from the nearby Pacific. With the city sound asleep, we'd be down in that buddha hall hours before sunrise, ripped to the tits on Chinese tea, warm energy flowing from the tai chi, sitting bolt upright in the chilly darkness and wrapped in our winter robes—like in the Buddhist Lecture Hall, there was no heat here either—and feeling more awake and alive than anyone could imagine. Even though we were sitting in what appeared to be a dungeon, we were filled with excitement, joy, and a sense of adventure, as if camping out on an ocean cliff. Often the meditation reminded me of being down at test depth in the submarine, listening to all the creeks and groans, wondering if I would stay alive, and thinking about eternity.

The historical Buddha and all the patriarchs of the Chan tradition had taught that the most important use of one's time was time spent on the meditation bench trying to still the mad mind. They said that there is more merit and virtue sitting in full lotus and trying to still one's mind than there is in building limitless temples throughout the universe.

Back at the Buddhist Lecture Hall, the hour-long sits had hurt like hell. I tried everything I could to survive the pain, and some of the diversions worked for a while, but it came always back. The master said that this pain was a necessary part of meditation, that it helped to melt away the bad karma gathered in a million eons. Each day as we wiped away this karma, our chances for enlightenment increased. Planting seeds of good karma by performing virtuous deeds and not being attached to the results even furthered our prospects.

Sure enough, after innumerable hours of sitting, the muscles and tendons in my legs gradually rearranged themselves. On occasions, I could sit the full hour in half lotus, even though it was painful, and every once in a while I could crank my legs up into full lotus for a few minutes. Still, the waves of false thought would arise from nowhere, and I continued to be lost in them. Helpless to stop this spurious flow, I indulged in trying to sort things out. I spent countless hours trying to make sense of my life, but the thoughts just continued to emerge like smoke from a fire. I'd follow one particle up until it disappeared, and then immediately grasp onto the next ash that came floating by. I tried regulating my breath, counting my breath, reciting special mantras, staring at the floor, rolling my eyeballs, and everything else I could think of, but my brain just kept smoking away.

Eventually, however, I discovered some techniques for clearing my mind. One was the sweeping Dharma. When thoughts popped up, rather than get lost in them, I'd brush them away. Sometimes the thoughts seemed quite profound, and indeed they were, but as far as meditation goes, they were just more dust, so I swept them away, and they lost their power over me. Another method was the laser beam. I envisioned my meditation as the source of the beam, and as thoughts arose, I blasted them with light—more or less like Luke Skywalker and the gang in *Star Wars*. I found myself gradually gaining perspective on my thoughts and began to experience some of the transcendental effects of meditation; no big deal, and not a major accomplishment, but certainly one of its more immediate rewards.

After a few months at Gold Mountain, during the second half of the hour-long sits, I started to feel the pain in my legs doing something positive for me. I don't know what chemical transformations were taking place, but it felt like a fire moving up my back and lapping at the edges of my brain. The master called it *kundalini* energy, the roused dragon. It was a very stimulating, tingling, massaging, and not at all displeasing feeling. This fire, or pain, could be used to center the intellect, and give one a feeling of transcendence. It was like looking down on top of the intellect instead of being wrapped up in it. Thoughts continued to arise, but instead of identifying with them, it was easier to just let them go.

At the time, I wasn't really aware of how these processes were working; all I knew was that we all were going through incredible changes in a very short period of time. I had truly quit both drinking and smoking. Considering that I'd been on the sauce ever since I was fourteen, and I'd suffered ten years of ever-increasing alcohol consumption, this was amazing. Suddenly, thanks to the master and the Buddhist teachings, it was all cut off, and I was drying out, detoxing, going cold turkey. No wonder my meditations were so confused for a while—my brain was in the process of purging itself of these old demons.

Those of us at Gold Mountain Monastery weren't just "studying" Buddhism; we were living it. And even though we were mere beginners, we were already reaping some of the rewards of practice. I was damn proud of myself—and greedy for more.

After several months of hard work, our renovation project was almost done. The buddha hall was the final touch—a place for ceremonies as well as for walking and sitting meditation. We laid out cheap green linoleum over the slab floor and painted the dusty old brick walls with a slushy cement mixture, sealing in all the dirt—it was the master's idea. The hall, which featured a high ceiling and only a couple of small windows, was quite dark and gloomy. Only the three gilded buddhas, huddled together in their glass case, showed any outward signs of life or hope; all else was drab and quiet. But I'd already learned that "all things are made from the mind alone," so I tried not to let any of this bother me.

We built meditation benches out of used lumber, covered them with foam and mustard-colored Naugahyde, and lined them around the perimeter of the hall. We filled the two center aisles with tiny bowing benches. One side of the hall was for men, the other for women, and we sat in meditation facing each other—not facing the wall, as in some monasteries. When the work was finished, a famous carver from Hong Kong, Mr. Wang, brought in an exquisitely beautiful eighteen-foot statue of Avalokiteshvara Bodhisattva, the bodhisattva of compassion, loaded with a thousand hands. Each hand had an eye carved in its palm, and many of the hands held magical instruments. The statue seemed especially beautiful to me. Because it hadn't been gilded yet, it didn't have every square inch of that wonderful dark and natural wood covered with gold paper. That would come later.

On all three floors we painted the wooden window frames canary yellow. From outside, the old brick building, with its ivy-covered walls and bright trim, looked pretty respectable. It must have emitted some kind of protective energy, because the neighborhood kids never broke our windows, while everyone else's were smashed regularly.

Finally, our new *bodhimandala*—our "home of enlightenment"—was finished. We had some great space to move about and cultivate. The nuns moved out of their apartment across town and into their new rooms on the second floor. The men had already taken the third floor, except for a couple of monks who determinedly slept sitting up in the buddha hall at night.

Having helped so much with the transformation of the building, I felt great pride, and a curious kind of identity with the building, almost as if it were alive. Here was a place where I really belonged, a special, magical home; a family. I felt supremely lucky that the master was working with all of us, and that we were all together in this one place.

It was during this ecstatic period that I began giving a lot of thought to leaving the home life and becoming a monk. The master had made it clear that all living beings possessed buddha nature, the innate potential for awakening, and that eventually, in some life or another, we could become enlightened. In the texts there were a few stories of laypeople getting enlightened, but it seemed that the best approach to realization was the total approach: becoming a monastic and devoting one's entire energy to the task.

I knew that being a monk involved renouncing everything. But what the hell? I wasn't married, I had no responsibilities except to myself, and my whole life was in transition. My life up until this point had been pretty meaningless, anyway. I wasn't doing myself any good, nor was I helping anyone else. I had lost contact with all my navy friends, and the commune I'd lived on had burned to the ground. Here at Gold Mountain, I could turn my back on the "red dust" and confusion of my past and start a new life. The Gold Mountain sangha members had twenty-four hours every day to meditate, study, practice, learn foreign languages, travel, and lecture on the Dharma.

Leaving home wasn't just something to think about: it was something one could do, an infinitely variable do-it-yourself salvation package. It was hands-on practice in a community of enlightenment, where everyone had access to three thousand years of collected wisdom, where everyone shared the same goal of attaining perfection in this very life, and where everyone supported each other along the path. In addition, while I was working out my own enlightenment, I could be an example for others, a field of blessings for the laypeople. Best of all, I'd get to be near the master: a fully accomplished teacher of true principles, a sage, a person without greed.

Listen, though, don't be fooled by all of this saint-like talk: there was a rather large gap, at the time, between my ideals and what I actually did. For instance, most of the cultivators, including the master, ate only one meal a day. I couldn't quite make that leap, so I ate a light breakfast every day with a couple of the other weak-minded laymen and downed a huge lunch alongside everybody. In the afternoons, when we weren't supposed to eat anything solid, I'd sometimes go out and get a thick milkshake—as thick as they could make it. The shake temporarily quenched my desire for dinner, as well as everything else I'd suppressed. Actually, I was quite surprised at the magnitude of my obsessive new desire for the shakes. I'd be OK for a while after lunch, but then the thought of them would start to knock at the door of my *hua tou*, the short phrase I was supposed to be using as the subject of my meditation. "Who is it that wants the milkshake? Why do I crave it so? Aren't I supposed to be getting rid of my desire mind?" Funny how all my desires—all my heavy black qi energy—was able to make a transference over to milkshakes.

The master frequently caught me eating when I wasn't supposed to, and while on some occasions he'd give me a big scolding, there was one inter- action with him that I'll never forget. This was on a day that I realized that not even the thickest milkshake was going to satiate my hunger. I ducked out, bought a big bag of gourmet pastries, and devoured all of them except for one apple pie—there just wasn't room for it in my stomach. Not wanting to be wasteful, I schlepped it into the monastery, rationalizing that I'd eat the pie the next morning. All during the evening lecture, however, I kept thinking of that delicious apple pie. (That must have been my undoing, sending all those juicy pie signals out. Any good submariner knows that you don't send out active pinging when you are trying to run silent and deep.) After the lecture, when everyone had turned in, I grabbed my pie, quietly crawled onto the fire escape from the bathroom window on the third floor, and climbed up to the roof. I didn't make a sound. The cool breeze blew in from the bay and stung my cheeks as I unwrapped the pie and took a huge bite.

At that exact moment, however, I turned and saw the master climbing up onto the roof. Momentarily stunned, I quickly mobilized myself and began walking in a big oval, as if I were up there doing walking meditation. The abbot started doing ovals too, except in the opposite direction. It was a large roof, but I still had a lot of pie in my mouth as we made our first pass.

"How does it feel?" the master inquired, quoting a popular Bob Dylan song and smiling his broad smile.

Well, I felt funny, wonderful, and weird. I had to laugh, and then I had to cry. My life had become so strange: here I was, in the middle of the night on a gravel rooftop doing circles with a Chinese abbot who was a living buddha, and for some reason he was using his energy to teach me, and his mind knew no bounds, and I felt loved and touched like I couldn't imagine. My heart was filled with faith, and I knew that my future in Buddhism would continue to be filled with unexpected wonders.

"It feels wonderful, Shifu!" I exclaimed (after I had swallowed the pie). Without saying another word, we both walked around for a bit, and then he climbed downstairs while I stayed up, trying to treasure the moment.

This story, which was ostensibly about greed, but really about the love between abbot and disciple, immediately became the master's favorite story, and later I would be asked to tell it over and over throughout the world. The Chinese especially loved it. "Kuo Yu, tell them about the pie!"

The milkshakes and pies, though, were actually the least of my problems. As a layman with an outside job, I had fallen into the habit of taking excursions in my old Chevy to places all around the Bay Area. I'd practice my Buddhism for a week or so, building up a bundle of light, blessings, and energy. Then, unable to help myself, I'd go out and binge on sensory delights, trying to hold on to at least the letter if not the spirit of the precepts. I'd never do anything really wrong; I'd just let some of my newfound light slip out, vanishing through the doors of the six senses. I'd fill my ears with rock and roll, my belly with sweet things to eat. As long as I wasn't drinking alcohol or smoking, I figured I was doing OK. After all, I was just a beginner, so there was no sense in being too hard on myself. I'd just let the car take me wherever it wanted to go. Nonetheless, it was always depressing to see my cultivation slip away.

Then one day I found myself heading north up Highway 1 toward Stinson Beach. It was classic warm California weather, and spring was in full bloom. The Deluxe Hardtop had a full tank of gas, all the windows were rolled down, and she was running like a Mercedes-Benz. The hitcher appeared almost as if planned, a wiry, long-haired sort wearing a trench coat and a vest. He hopped in and immediately asked if I wanted to smoke a joint. I told him I didn't like to smoke in the car—someone might notice.

"No problem," he said. "Just take one now, and enjoy it later." He opened up both sides of his vest, revealing a multitude of hand-sewn pockets, each one holding little packs of marijuana cigarettes. It was a one-man traveling dope delicatessen. I hadn't smoked in months—I was supposed to be following the precepts!—but this was an offer I couldn't refuse.

"I've got Acapulco Gold, Havana Red, Mellow Yellow, Colombian, and some really far-out local stuff," he said proudly.

I accepted a large home-grown number and delivered the hitchhiker to his destination. Then, with an excited and familiar feeling in my gut—the knowledge that I was soon going to be smoking some weed (and breaking some rules)—I drove the car up a dirt road that led me to the top of a vast grassy hill overlooking the Pacific. The sun was just setting, and the sky was brilliant red when I fired up that fat joint and took a hit.

Man—that was all it took! I exploded into empty space. My head ceased to exist, and my mind shot up, expanding in a million directions, merging with the universe. I was a thousand feet tall! My thoughts were everywhere! I was aware of a tiny body standing down on top of that hill. I knew it was me, but everything else was me, too. It was wild and wonderful, and I delighted in it for a few minutes.

Then suddenly I was completely terrified. I'd smoked pot plenty of times, but nothing like this had ever happened—this was out of control. Buddhism had taken away my limits, but I wanted to come down. I beseeched the buddhas, telling them I was grateful for the experience and that it meant a lot to me, but I wasn't quite ready to stay that way. I needed more development. I just wanted to go back to being my normal old self. I promised them if they would just let me return to my body, I would cultivate like hell, follow the rules, and quickly attain buddhahood. I remained in this altered state for about a half hour, half enjoying it, half scared to death. Then gradually I returned to normal. Shaking and sweating, I got in the car and returned to the temple.

The next night, at the end of his formal sutra lecture, the master asked if anyone had any "special states" they wanted to share. Having been void of any interesting states for quite some time, and without thinking of the consequences, I leapt at the chance to describe my recent experience.

"Shifu," I said, "I had a state where I left my body, and my mind ascended into empty space. I felt like I was everywhere at the same time, and that I was part of everything in the universe."

I surveyed the room; all the women were staring at me in deep admiration and the men looked sick with jealousy (that's how it appeared to me, anyway). I had completely neglected, however, to mention anything about the toke of dope. The master just nodded.

"Anyone else?"

The next morning, I started feeling incredibly guilty about not telling the whole truth, the absolute truth, and nothing but the truth. Mea culpa. I wasn't going to get anywhere in this holy-man business being a liar or telling half-truths. And the big fat lie wasn't going to undo itself—it hung in my face, showing no sign of going away. Throughout the day the size of my lie grew astronomically until it was all I could think about. I shuddered when I thought of making the requisite and embarrassing public apology, but I didn't see any other recourse. I would certainly never get enlightened with this monstrous offense sitting on my conscience.

Why couldn't the Buddhists have private little confessionals like the Catholics? No, we had to do it out in front of Shifu and everybody. *OK, OK, OK already*, I said to myself. *I'll get it straightened out.*

That evening, after the ceremonies and before the lecture, I offered incense and then crawled down on my hands and knees before the master and the rest of the community and made my public confession. I told them that I actually did experience that incredible state I was talking about, but I neglected to mention, in all fairness, one small detail. I took one little toke on a marijuana cigarette before the experience. I was sure, however, that the experience was due more to my spiritual cultivation than it was the drug.

The audience tittered and snickered. Some of the ex-dopers burst out laughing. The master, however, handled the situation very tactfully, appreciating, I am sure, how much I had already suffered, and let me off with a gentle warning to try to do things according to the rules in the future. He promised that then I would start having genuine experiences.

I was not quite through breaking the rules, however. There was one thing I knew I had to take care of before I could fully release my grasp upon the conditioned world. I knew this so deep down that it filled my body on every level—except the conscious one. I was just barely able to keep the thought out.

One evening, at dusk, while driving around San Francisco in search of the perfect milkshake, I saw her standing there, an apparition, on the side entrance to the freeway. She was a tall, shapely woman with long golden hair, a white blouse, and a gray skirt, and her thumb was up, like Tom Robbins's cowgirl with the blues. I immediately pulled over, feeling as if all this were meant to be, and threw open the passenger door.

"You going near the airport?" she asked as she slid in next to me.

"Uh, yes. I'm going in that direction," I said, struggling to keep my eyes on her face. She did have a strikingly beautiful one: prominent cheekbones, a long, slender aquiline nose, lips like scarlet rose petals, and cobalt eyes that glowed in the evening dusk. She must have been in her early twenties.

"I've got to see if I can find my boyfriend. He's coming in from Alaska. He just got out of jail, and I'm supposed to meet him." I slipped the Deluxe into drive and punched it. It responded as if I'd stepped on a ripe tomato.

"What flight is he coming in on?" I asked.

"That's just it," she said. "I'm not sure."

My hands gripped the wheel tightly. I could feel trembling emanating from the core of my reactor—I had to force myself to be calm. We exchanged polite chitchat all the way to the airport, but the atomic attraction between the two of us was something words could not describe. My blood pressure was off the scale.

When we arrived at San Francisco International, I sensed that her attempt to locate her friend might fail, so I offered to wait while she looked around. As I sat in the car watching the people come and go, I asked myself what in the hell I was doing. This had to be an illusion—it was surely a major test. Maybe it was a bodhisattva, an enlightened being. In any case, she was too good to be true. She would never come back. And if she did, then what? None of this was part of the Master Plan to attain enlightenment and help all sentient beings. Oh well—I couldn't think about it anymore. To think would bring my desires into the realm of consciousness, and then of course Shifu would be able to hear me thinking. If I didn't think, perhaps I'd be all right. I could think about it tomorrow. This radiant being wasn't going to come out anyway. I'd just been used.

The door from United flew open and out she came walking out like every man's dream, her hair blowing gently in the evening breeze. I couldn't believe it—she was walking back to me!

"He's not there," she said, and smiled. "It doesn't matter, anyway. I just wanted to get some money that he owes me. I think he's traveling with some girl. He might have changed airlines." I had no idea what was going on with her search for her friend, but I was really glad she hadn't found him.

"Well, uh, where you going?" I asked. "I've got some time. I suppose I could take you where you want to go."

She slid in a bit closer to me than before, her silky, perfect legs sliding out from her skirt. I'd forgotten all about my mission for milkshakes. Now my entire body was doing a low-level shake. I was overwhelmed with desire.

"Well, I guess I'll go back to San Francisco. I've got some friends there I can stay with," she said.

We drove out of the airport, heading north on the Bayshore Freeway. Something had to happen soon, I figured, or this incredible opportunity was going to vanish. I couldn't use words. I'd never really learned the fine art of how to pick up women, but apparently it wasn't going to be necessary. She looked at me, I looked at her—the Deluxe, running in automatic, took the next right off the freeway and found its way into a large grassy lot behind an industrial complex next to the bay. No one was around. It was dark, and the sky was full of a thousand stars. We got out and kissed, my mind spinning out of control into those soft luscious lips. A cool breeze fanned us and the knee-high grass swayed back and forth. I was vaguely aware of cars passing on the freeway, but we were removed from it all. I didn't know who this woman was—I didn't even know her name, and it seemed irrelevant to ask. She didn't know me either, yet we really did know each other; we were like mountain cats meeting for the first time on some distant mountain. We melted into the grass and made love.

Afterward, I held her, and we watched the stars in the night sky. When it was time to go, I glanced at my watch. It was exactly seven thirty. I felt sure that Shifu was watching from the sky.

I dropped my dream apparition off in the city and returned to Gold Mountain Monastery with dread in my heart and fear in my bones. Oh, well. What was done was done. I'd put it behind me and move forward with my life. I rang the bell, and one of the other students let me in.

"How's it going?" I asked nervously.

"OK."

"What's happening?" I inquired, trying to act nonchalant.

"Shifu called," he replied.

"Oh? What did he have to say?" It felt like a large stone had manifested in my gut.

"He asked about you."

"Oh! What time did he call?" I asked.

"Seven thirty."

My God! That was exactly when I looked at my watch and wondered if he was watching me from the sky.

"What did he say?" I asked.

"Tell Kuo Yu that when crossing the sea of suffering, don't stop to drink the salt water!"

I walked upstairs and crawled into my sleeping box. The final great mortal sin had been completed, and as far as I was concerned, was signed, sealed, and delivered. It was over. It was out of my system and done with.

The layman had been laid. There would be no confessing this one to the Great Assembly. No, it would be a secret kept between me and my Shifu, and I would repay his kindness for allowing me this one infidelity, for not broadcasting this momentary indiscretion, by devoting the rest of my life to upright, proper, moral service of the Dharma. Yes, that's how I would handle it!

8. MONKHOOD

For months I'd been entertaining the idea of leaving the home life, but I still hadn't made a decision. The abbot, in hints subtle and not so subtle, had made it clear that the best way for some of us to reach enlightenment was to leave home and become monks or nuns. Every week he told stories of how each of the patriarchs first left home and then later became enlightened. At Gold Mountain it was clear that the left-home people got all the attention, while the laymen played second fiddle. But I didn't know if I had the confidence to go through with it. I had spent most of my life as a drinker and a doper. Could I really commit myself to the spiritual life? If the master were to give me the go-ahead, I decided, if he told me that I had the deep roots and wisdom to do the job, then I would leave home. I reckoned that since he could see the future, I could probably cajole him into giving me a glimpse, and perhaps then I'd see what was in store for me.

One day I finally mustered up the guts to ask the master whether or not I should leave the home life. I got down on my knees before him and popped the big one.

"Shifu, should I become a monk, or should I remain a layman?" I inquired.

The master was not baited. He took a long draw from his cup of tea, shifted around in his seat to get a little more comfortable, and with a mind centered in true suchness and the voice of Jack Nicholson, replied, "Kuo Yu, if you were to drop dead right now, I could bring you back to life. But as far as answering your question about leaving the home life, I can't help you. You have to make that decision yourself."

On September 22, 1972, at Gold Mountain Monastery in the city of San Francisco, without the consent or blessing of my parents, nor the knowledge of any of my old friends, I took the vows of a novice monk, just as all the patriarchs had done throughout history. I shaved my head and was given the robes of a Buddhist monk. The master presided over the ceremony, and three of us made our vows. (Later on, we would take the complete precepts of full ordination there in Gold Mountain Monastery and become the first Americans in our tradition to do so on American soil.) There was Irving, a newcomer with a degree in Chinese studies, and Judy, a bright young woman studying for her doctorate in Sanskrit at the University of California. And then there was me, an ex-submarine sailor turned idealistic and wastrel hippie. With little fanfare or recognition, we left home, formally dedicating our lives to the achievement of buddhahood for ourselves and for all living beings. Together the three of us knelt with palms joined and, following the master's lead, recited our vows three times over, while the senior monks and nuns placed three rows of incense on our heads, scarring our waiting flesh with the universal marks of a left-home person. When the twelve red coals of incense reached my skin, the pain raged along the top of my crown and throughout my brain, while rivers of tears ran involuntarily down my cheeks.

After the smoke settled and the others had gone to their rooms, I walked around the temple in a daze. I felt off balance, light of weight, and lost. My hair was gone, my street clothes were gone, my identity was gone. Suddenly, I didn't know who the hell I was anymore.

During my first months as a novice monk, I was completely depressed. Not since I had become a sailor had I undergone such a rapid change of identity. I liked the idea of cultivating the Way and all that, but I hated being different from everyone else. I'd given away my car, so I no longer had the freedom I'd enjoyed as a layman. I didn't like being isolated and alone all that much. And with robes, I couldn't just casually walk into stores and order milkshakes, even though I still had a strong desire to. Furthermore, I found I was just as attracted to women as a celibate monk than I had been as a layman. The three poisons of greed, hatred, and stupidity continued to rule my mind. It was gradually beginning to sink in what I'd done—I had just given up my entire life to become an ascetic. I was adrift in the sea of human suffering and far from home. With no escape mechanisms remaining, life at the monastery became increasingly difficult.

One beautiful San Francisco day we were celebrating the feast of Avalokiteshvara Bodhisattva's accomplishment of the Way. We spent the better part of the morning cooped up inside the buddha hall performing Chinese ceremonies, with all the bells, gongs, drumming, and pounds of sandalwood incense being offered up to the sky. The Cantonese lay ladies—their husbands usually stayed home—had stacked the altars with plate-loads of fruit, cookies, dim sum, rice cakes, and other delicacies. At noon we enjoyed a vegetarian feast.

After lunch, the master sat on a bench in the buddha hall surrounded by a dozen laypeople. They seemed so gay and cheerful. Of course they were happy; they got to go home after all of this. But we, the American sangha, deeply searching for the meaning of life, stood like statues, more or less mindlessly performing the interminable Chinese ceremonies.

On that particular day, a huge depression set in. After lunch, when all the happy-go-lucky laymen got up to leave, I was stuck with a mountain of dirty dishes. I was morose, heavy-hearted, dismal, down in the dumps, dogged by the sudden realization that it would be twenty-four hours until the next meal.

My buddy and fellow novice, Brother Irving, was clearing the tables. He looked as sad as I felt, walking around with his face down, practically hitting the floor. As I began the monumental task of washing the dishes, I indulged in false thinking. This wasn't turning out like I'd imagined monastic life to be. It seemed most everyone here was greedy for power, position, respect, purity, or psychic phenomena, myself included. Where was the brotherly love?

I was also having my doubts about Buddhism. Sometimes it seemed like a giant three-thousand-year-old attic that needed clearing out. (Perhaps I was just the one to do it—except no one was interested in what I had to say, and I didn't know how to go about doing it, anyway.) And I had plenty of doubts about my own ability to cultivate the Way. I didn't have doubts about the master. He was the real article. But how was anyone like me going to become a patriarch like him? It seemed impossible.

I was slaving away at the sink as Irving brought over more and more dishes, stacking them in tall piles on the counter to my right. With hands submerged in the murky water, I sunk deeper into self-pity and despair. The master hadn't been paying any attention to me lately, and I hadn't seen any psychic fireworks in a while. When was this good-karma business going to start paying off? My life felt like murky dishwater, a big waste. I was stuck in this monastery, a big nothing. I was a monk, so it was my job to go nowhere, but I wasn't very good at that, either. I wasn't getting anywhere in my meditation.

Oh well, I thought. *What's the use? I'll never get enlightened.* My life was tragically wasted, and there wasn't a person in the world who cared about me. With a big lump in my throat, I was choking back tears when the master appeared beside me. He looked wild and intense, his eyes gleaming.

"Why you go to breaking all these dishes?" he yelled.

I was completely confused. I didn't know what he was talking about.

"These dishes costing lot of moneys! What wrong with you? We no can afford broken dishes!"

I hadn't broken any dishes, ever. I hadn't broken any today, or any time in the past, not one since I'd been in the monastery. The abbot was out of his mind.

"Shifu, I haven't broken any dishes!" I exclaimed.

"Why you go to breaking all these dishes?" he yelled again. My doubts about being there expanded with each repetition of the abbot's strange words.

"These dishes cost lots of moneys. Too much breaking dishes!" he yelled for the last time, and then he was gone.

I stared into the water. Here I had just left the home life, left behind all that had mattered, and was dedicating my life to some remote ideal of enlightenment and the bitterly ascetic lifestyle that it entailed, and my teacher had gone off the deep end. As I wallowed in my jumbled thoughts, I happened to catch, out of the corner of my eye, a glimpse of the towering stacks of dishes. Irving had just brought in another load, building up a huge pyramid, which he had carelessly placed on top of a large round-bottomed wok. The top dish started to waver. Then it started to wobble. Irving was on his way back into the dining hall when the top dish slid and set off an avalanche. Like collapsing dominoes, stack after stack, the dishes crashed down into the sink and onto the kitchen floor all around me. Over two dozen bowls and plates were broken.

Although I hadn't touched a thing, I was the only one around when it happened. The doors from the buddha hall flung open, and crowds of people came running in to stare. I stood in shock as it dawned on me what had just happened. The abbot had just told me about an unexpected, totally unpredictable event that was going to happen in the future. Then it had actually happened—again. My brain reeled, trying to get a grip on the situation. I knew beyond a doubt by now that Shifu could read my mind, that he could literally and clearly see into the future. I had seen enough to convince me: he knew. He had known that I'd been crying for help.

It was the birthday of Avalokiteshvara Bodhisattva, the magical being with a thousand hands and thousand eyes who is able to hear the cries of humans in distress. All one has to do is call her name and she will manifest in the world, sometimes as an ordinary person. I had called her name, and something crazy had happened—I had gotten a response. Now I was weeping with joy. Something inconceivably wonderful was happening to me!

From that day, the seed of faith I had in the master took solid root. In the old days in China, a student would sometimes kneel outside the monastery gate for two or three days to demonstrate his sincerity. At Gold Mountain, in the heart of the American ghetto, one would not likely live for the two or three days, so sincerity had to be shown in other ways. With Shifu, exterior acts of sincerity didn't work unless they were matched with a commensurate amount of internal sincerity. I discovered for myself that if I was sincere, the master was there for me, and guidance came in some form or another. I prayed for his help constantly. He didn't fix things for me, but he showed me how to act. With him by my side, I felt there was no trial I couldn't overcome—even this monk business.

Then again, there *were* problems that even Shifu couldn't solve. Gold Mountain, despite all of the spiritual progress being made, was still a bunch of afflicted humans all living together, and sometimes things got heated. I was still just a fresh young novice when the monks and the nuns somehow became involved in a long, drawn-out fight over who would run the monastery.

Shifu spared no efforts in teaching and transforming his female students, and spent countless thousands of hours showing them the Way. In return, the nuns were fiercely loyal and very hardworking. They held the same difficult schedule that we did, did everything that we did, and outperformed us in many ways, especially in sheer volume of translated materials.

But the nuns at Gold Mountain had their share of problems and then some. Traditionally, women in Buddhism were placed secondary to men, a reflection of the cultures Buddhism had passed through during its long history. In America the feminist movement was just starting to gather steam, and yet the American women at Gold Mountain had taken a step three thousand years back in time. They had to follow the men in line; had to live on the second floor below the men. They even had to bow to any monk, although they went out of their way to avoid it (except, of course, to bow to the master). A fully ordained bhikshuni observed 348 rules, while a bhikshu only had to worry about 250. I believe that in one of the old commentaries it even said that the abbot of a monastery had to scold the nuns once a day, just on general principle.

I think it all started when one nun, Tall & Thin, probably frustrated with this unfair situation and with trying to deal with us guys, made a vow never to speak to men again. Unfortunately she was in the middle of a cooperative translation effort of some of the master's recent sutra lectures, and it involved working with the monks. They could talk to her, but they had to guess what she wanted to say, and if they got it right she would kind of nod her head in approval.

Then some of the women got tired of being whacked and poked by the monks when they were nodding off during meditation periods. Things deteriorated from there. Shifu tried to equalize matters by giving control of the temple funds to the women. The money quickly became a control issue. The nuns had the money, and we had to ask them for it whenever we needed to conduct temple business. And though I could hardly blame them, they didn't make it easy. Because of this friction between the men and women, there was plenty of affliction going around.

One day it was my turn to give a little Dharma chat while we were all sitting in a meditation session, the women sitting bolt upright facing the men, with thirty feet of cold floor between us. I was telling the story of the apple pie, how I was up on the roof when I suddenly looked over and saw "this old Chinese man" climbing up the ladder.

Upon hearing these words, Tall & Thin jumped up out of her seat and screamed, "You can't call our Shifu an old man!"

Jesus Christ! I didn't know what she was talking about. I'd somehow offended her, and suddenly she was raging at me right in the middle of my Dharma speech. This was a hell of a time for her to decide to talk to men! Heck, I wasn't being disrespectful of Shifu. At the time, I hadn't realized who it was at first; it really just looked like an old Chinese man climbing a ladder. But the nun perceived matters differently, and she laid into me hard. I was not unmoved. In fact, I was very moved, hurt, and injured. I terminated my speech early, and at the next break ran upstairs and locked myself into an empty room for a couple of days.

During that time I didn't eat, didn't answer my door, and didn't come out. I did, however, take some pain pills, and wished that I were dead. I figured I'd just stay there until my body got underway on nuclear power like the yogis or something. Actually, I was waiting for Shifu to rescue me, but he didn't seem to be going for it. Finally, hungry and burned out after the third day, I came out and started attending ceremonies. At the next evening lecture, Shifu addressed the root of my problem. "You can't expect everyone to like you when you start to get ahead. Some people will become obstructed when they see you making progress. They will try to pull you down. But you don't have to go down. You can be unmoved in this small, small, smallest of affairs. Next time try it out. Once you let yourself go down, however, no one can save you."

One night not too long after this, I overheard the elder monks plotting ways to get rid of the nuns entirely. They had all gathered in an abandoned room in the back of the building, and since the walls were thin—half the thickness of normal walls—it was easy to overhear them. They thought that a monastery should be for men. Since they had gone to all the trouble of giving up women, they figured they shouldn't have to live with them. Why have all the hassles of a marriage and yet none of the benefits? They decided to hold a bogus "board meeting" the next day when they knew there would be few nuns around. They would bring up a bunch of petty charges and then hold a quick vote to see if the nuns would be allowed to stay in the monastery. The nuns, of course, wanted to stay in the monastery because they liked only to be near their Shifu, and they didn't want the annoyance of having to commute to work. The next day, however, the meeting was held, and the nuns were voted out of the monastery.

The laypeople were appalled by this behavior. Luckily, a few months later a wealthy and generous layman donated his nearby mansion to the monastery, and Shifu told the nuns they could live there. And to meet the challenge of women's liberation, the master came up with a new rule. Instead of men always being senior, he said that we would no longer measure people by how long a period of time they spent in the monastery, nor whether they were men or women. Instead they would be measured by their Dharma nature; whoever had wisdom would be the leader. After that, life for everyone settled down a lot.

Months passed by at Gold Mountain, and although our collective afflictions had calmed, my own personal afflictions still needed a lot of work. All of my bad habits had pretty much banded together in one area: greed. (Most of the other American cultivators were having trouble with it, too.) I was especially greedy for food. I'm sure that if I didn't have a good teacher this greed would have manifested as greed for sex, wine, drugs, or any number of things that would help me to scatter and disperse myself, but for the time being food seemed to do the job.

My greed landed me the cook's job at the monastery. I stir-fried vegetables and baked whole-grain bread for the sangha. I put out a damn good spread, but I couldn't stick to just one meal a day. I needed more. I nibbled, I sampled, I tasted.

My greed for sweets in particular astonished me. I craved sugar, sought it out, and consumed it in massive quantities. When I reached my fill, my head swam in confusion, my worries and problems temporarily disappearing in a whirling haze—together with all my spiritual progress. I knew this was just a temporary relief valve for my freshly cut-off outflows. The master often counseled, "Slowly, slowly, slowly—don't try to do it all at once." But trying to control my greed for food was like trying to stop a flooding river. I vowed over and over again to eat only once a day, but, it seemed, to no avail.

To be fair, it wasn't just my lack of self-discipline that was contributing to the problem; it was obvious that none of us living at Gold Mountain were getting proper nutrition. We ate scraps of leftovers from the farmer's market, as well as stuff rummaged out of dumpsters. There was never any consistency. One time we got a real bonus in the food department when a restaurant across town started giving us huge boxes of their leftover donuts. Every morning, the nuns picked them up on their way in to the temple, dropping them off on the marble counter. The "'nuts," as we called them, seemed impossible to ignore. After the morning meditation, several of us, both men and women, gathered around the galley to investigate the donuts. It wasn't long before we abandoned our vows about not eating before noon. Well, we rationalized, these were not precepts, just additional vows taken on to enhance cultivation. Even some of the nuns, who usually put on a much better show of following the rules, were moved by the 'nuts and were seen snitching them on the sly. I supposed a person could be forgiven for over-vowing him- or herself and then slacking off just a hair. Anyway, it was great fun committing this smallest of infractions, and the master, I rationalized, was giving his sanction, because he never said anything about it. Perhaps he looked upon it as an expedient Dharma. I imagined him saying, "Let them eat donuts!"

At lunchtime we'd really pork out. It wasn't long, of course, before we became sick of the donuts, and even sicker of our addiction—but we continued to devour them. I was so depressed over my lack of willpower that I tried to break my addiction by going on a fast. I didn't eat a thing for three days and drank nothing but water. I was in agony most of the time, thinking about nothing but glazed and buttermilk donuts. I broke my fast with five of them, and the rush of sugar almost killed me. Finally, the nuns just stopped bringing the donuts in. We all went into deep withdrawal— but were glad they were gone.

Our troubles with craving, however, were far from over. One morning, while out on a brisk jog, I happened upon a Big Hunk factory, just three blocks from the monastery on Market Street. I was surprised to see they still made these things, which I'd loved dearly as a kid. Big Hunks consisted of a white taffy-like nougat embedded with peanuts. If they were cold you could shatter them into pieces on the sidewalk; once warm, they pulled the fillings right out of your teeth. And now I'd discovered the universal source of Big Hunks, right in our own backyard.

At night the factory threw their rejects into a dumpster in the alley. After my run, I'd grab a couple dozen bars and bring them back to the kitchen. Layman Guffaw was the first to get hooked. He even took over the dumpster digging when I tried to give it up, arguing that we couldn't let this food go to waste.

My system became so out of balance from all this abuse that I got sick. Since it never occurred to me to ask for help—to ask for my needs to be met in a direct manner—I got even sicker. My stomach could no longer stomach what I was putting so violently into it. At lunchtime I always ate too much, and since there were no healthy flora and fauna down there to aid with the digestion, it all wanted to come back up. One day, after hitting my absolute lowest sugar bottom, I found a five-gallon bucket and took it up to the roof and puked my guts out, vomiting a veritable volcano of junk food. I left the bucket up on the roof and continued to go up and barf every afternoon until it was full. Then I had to get another bucket, and soon it was full, too. I realized I had to do something with them, so one night I waited until everyone was meditating, then I snuck up to the roof, got my buckets, and dumped them across the street. This strange behavior went on for two or three months before I finally summoned the courage to stop eating the Hunks.

During this difficult time as a new monk, my favorite escape was taking the trolley out to the ocean beach at the end of the avenues. There, with my slipper-like shoes in my pockets, I could walk in the surf and feel Buddha's eternal ocean lapping at my feet. Out there in the warm sand and cool sea breezes I did a lot of starting over, a lot of sincere internal repenting, talking to the master and any buddhas or bodhisattvas who were willing to listen. Yes, I was doing OK, limiting the drop in my falls, and always returning to cultivation with fresh resolve, but I was having a rough go of it. To make up for my little slips, I'd generate fresh vows, and sometimes sear incense marks on my flesh to make them stick. One time, I burned three quarter-size circles on my left wrist to seal vows I made to the buddhas: to eat only one meal a day, to always sleep sitting up at night, and to leave the home life in every lifetime. On another occasion, I burned a swastika pattern on my belly—not the Nazi emblem, but the ancient Buddhist character *wan*, which indicated that "the ten thousand things were all simultaneously one."

Walking the beach, away from the cold cement walls of the monastery, gave me some perspective on my situation. Everywhere I saw suffering: the hopelessness of the Haight, the misery of the Mission, the toughness of the Tenderloin, the drugs, the dirty sidewalks, the iron gratings over all the windows and doors. I wasn't missing anything by being a monk.

But there was one particular experience that really helped me get through my beginning times of being ordained—going to jail. This is how it happened:

I occasionally used the temple car to pick up Shifu, go to the printers, or run miscellaneous errands. In the process I managed to accrue a lot of parking tickets. I didn't pay them much attention because I figured that what we were doing was tremendously important for the world, and we didn't have time to be bothered with minutia—we'd simply transcend these minor annoyances because the Buddha was on our side. Apparently the city of San Francisco didn't see things quite the same way, because they kept sending us notices, notices, and more notices on the overdue tickets. When they finally sent an order to appear in court, I figured it was time to deal with the problem. I'd just go down there, see the judge, and when he saw me and understood the nature of the situation, he'd undoubtedly let me off the hook. What else could he do? I was a monk; I didn't have any money.

Instead, he gave me a five-day jail sentence, though he said I could break the sentence up and serve my time on two weekends, and he allowed me to go back to the temple to get my affairs in order. I was weirdly excited about it, although I don't know exactly why. Was the monastery really so bad that I looked forward to going to the cooler? No, I was stimulated about the prospects of a fresh adventure, a new challenge, a chance to be out from under the big monks. I'd been cooped up so long that even going to prison sounded like a pleasant diversion.

I approached the master and told him about the situation. His counsel was that I should turn this situation around. Under no condition should I lie down while at the jail; I should continue with my practice of sleeping sitting up. Also, he added, I should eat only one meal a day, at noon, and be sure not to eat any of the prison meat.

The bus ride from downtown San Francisco out to the Contra Costa county jail was almost a treat. It was no Greyhound, mind you. The seats were hard and the windows dirty, but I still had a splendid view of the whole South Bay Area as we bounced along, my fellow prisoners and I, on our way to the calaboose. It felt wonderful just to let go of the controls and turn my life over to the government for a few days.

Once at prison, they confiscated my robes and gave me some prison clothing—dungaree tops and bottoms—but I was allowed to keep my slipper shoes, which I fondly called my arhat shoes. Then they marched us in and gave us showers. All of this was in public, with lots of guards and prisoner-helpers yelling at us every step of the way. After the shower they sprayed us with chemicals to kill bugs, whether we had any or not. Then I was taken to my cell in a block on the second floor.

The prison was divided into three floors, each with two wings, making a total of six cell blocks. Each cell block probably had fifty or a hundred cells—I'm not sure how many—but they ran along each wall, and the center area in between was designated a "day area." I shared a cell with this terribly afflicted guy who had the lower rack. His face was all red, and he looked like he was extremely angry all the time. When they served him his food he grumbled and swore and threw most of it into the toilet. I tried talking to him a couple of times, but he had nothing to say to me.

I spent the first afternoon and evening in my cell. I slept sitting up, listening to the sounds of suffering and lament from all around. Finally, an hour or so after lights out, the place settled down and everybody slept. The next morning I was allowed out of my cell for some "yard time." Since I was 6'4" tall and sported a freshly shaved head, no one messed with me. I walked around, acting like I belonged there, which I guess I did. Perhaps they thought I was a white supremacist racist or a criminally insane murderer. I let most of them think their thoughts, but I did let a couple of people know I was just there for parking tickets. I picked up the lingo fast. Every sentence began with "Hey, man!"

That evening, back in my cell and up on my bunk, I locked into full lotus for meditation. Inmates were still out in the day area, however, and curiosity drew them near. When I looked up from my trance, I saw four of them hanging on my door.

"What's he doing, man?" one of them asked.

"He's meditating, man!" another answered. I decided to hold my ground. I felt the protective envelope of the buddhas and bodhisattvas around me. All systems were on full alert, but I was not scared.

"Let's see how well he can meditate," said the first one, and he began to light matches and throw them at me. I tripled my concentration, silently working on the *Great Compassion Mantra*, projecting this powerful spell out at my fellow sufferers. My whole being was full of energy; I was putting out so much of it I thought I might start levitating. The matches and insults continued to fly, but nothing could touch me. I kept sitting, and eventually my tormentors went away. Later that night after lockup, I heard lots of talk about me.

"Hey man, is he still sitting in there?"

"Yeah, man, he's doing his yoga, man. Be cool!"

"Hey, that's far-out stuff. He's probably not even here, man."

As I sat there enjoying the cool night air wafting in from my window, I realized that once again, the master's instructions were paying off. I'd been here only one day, and already I had the respect of many of the inmates—I'd even taught them a thing or two. What amazed me was that none of this jail stuff bothered me. In fact I was enjoying my experience.

The next week before I went back, the master asked me if I thought I could fast for the two remaining days of my sentence. I told him I could, and we discussed our plan of attack. Once again I took the bus ride out to the county jail to finish off my obligation to the city of San Francisco. In the early afternoon of the first day, while I was out walking in the day area, I passed a group of eight or nine guys sitting in a circle on the shiny floor. One of them looked up at me and said, "Say, man, could we ask you a question?"

"Sure, what is it?" I replied.

"Where did you get those shoes?"

"These are arhat shoes," I replied. "We wear these in the monastery where I come from."

"What are you, some kind of a monk or something?"

"Yeah, I'm an American Buddhist monk," I said. "A bhikshu."

"Well, what are you in here for?" he asked.

"I got a whole bunch of parking tickets, and since I don't have any money, they gave me five days."

"Jesus, that's something! Are we glad to hear that! We were wondering about you. Sorry man, didn't mean to bother you."

"No problem," I said.

The next day, this same group flagged me down as I was walking in the yard, and started asking questions about Buddhism and the monastery. I knew they were going to ask, and I was ready for them. I told them they could make the best use of their time here if they thought of this place as a monastery and not a jail. I was really cranked up. In some ways, I told them, this is even better than a monastery. You can sleep a lot more, since you don't have to work or follow a strict schedule. You can use your sentence to completely turn your life around, or you can just waste this precious time and sit around stewing in your own crap and blaming all your problems on everyone else. All things are made from the mind alone. Start cultivating the Way. The sea of suffering is endless, but with one turn you can swim for the other shore of nirvana. I showed them how to fold their legs into half and full lotus, and instructed them in meditation.

When my sentence was up, I walked out on a cloud, stomach empty, spirit soaring, and feeling like I'd really accomplished something. This was it! I had stumbled upon the big one—there was nothing higher. I'd reached the peak of human experience. Well, not yet, but it was within my grasp.

9. CREATING BUDDHAS

The Chinese have a saying that the way to obtain the most powerful poison is to get all the various poisonous creatures—snakes, scorpions, spiders, and so forth—put them in a box, and let them sort things out for themselves. When you came back and found the one remaining, it would have the supreme poison.

As time went on, our situation began to feel kind of like the time of the Sixth Patriarch, when some deluded monks were ready to kill for the Dharma. I'd already forgotten my dream of everyone holding hands and acting like a love commune or a bunch of jolly Christians working together happily ever after. Instead, it was beginning to seem like at Gold Mountain, it was every man for himself.

For instance, there was Irving, my dishwashing friend, who had left home at the same time that I did. Heng Irving was very industrious. He had a degree in Chinese studies from a college back East, and every day worked diligently on his translations, his favorite a book of short stories and poems about the Venerable Master Hsu Yun. I especially admired Irving for his abilities to sit in full lotus for long periods of time. His lay name was Kuo Tao, the Result of the Way, and I think the big monks were jealous of it, because Irving was regularly singled out and picked on. I think they were also jealous of his ability to sit and to translate, and of the attention he occasionally received from the master—they were used to having it all.

Eventually Irving couldn't take it anymore and moved from the temple out into the garden, a long, narrow, forty-inch strip of dirt behind the back of the buddha hall. At the end of this muddy little path, crammed in by three walls, Irving built a meditation hut from scraps of wood. His meditation hut was just big enough to sit in, and there, when not involved with group functions, he lived.

It also seemed that the more you advanced in your practice, the more critical the master became of you: pointing out your faults, chipping away at your ego. A good example of this was Kent, number one apostle and the master's right-hand man. He was a natural because he'd lived in Taiwan as an officer in the United States Navy, submarine service, and had traveled the Taiwanese countryside in his spare time. On one of his outings he'd visited an old monk who lived on top of one of the mountains, high above the tea and pineapple plantations. The old monk was called the "Fruit Monk" because all he ate was fruit and nuts. He was an old cultivator who never lay down, and somehow he always knew who was coming up the mountain before they got there. Kent was deeply moved by this experience, and it was one of the seeds that caused his desire to cultivate to sprout. At Gold Mountain he quickly picked the Mandarin language back up, and added to his repertoire the enchanting philosophical words of Buddhism. He held a degree in English from Harvard and had just finished his master's at Stanford when he left the home life. He studied poetry, Chinese astrology, the *I Ching*, and enjoyed the finest Chinese teas. He had an unusual interest in plumbing, mainly because he had never done any. He was also a workaholic. He suffered a dichotomy in that all he ever talked about was going off somewhere to hibernate and just sit in meditation all day, but in reality he simply loved to work. He liked people and was happiest when in the midst of them. He became heavily involved with the refugee program and worked as an ad hoc lawyer to help countless Chinese and Vietnamese naturalize into the United States. This involved a lot of work down at city hall and a lot of high-powered running around. On the Buddhist lecture circuit, he translated for the master and often gave his own talks. He was believable and powerful. He quite naturally rose to the top, and before long was wearing red robes, signifying that he was the ceremonial leader of the monastery.

Kent did, however, have his share of problems. I'm not really sure what they were all about. It seems he had a funny little quirk, a way of complicating things, making some of his working relationships a bit sticky and dysfunctional. In any case, the master let him run his course—at first. But of course it was only a matter of time before Kent set himself up for a big Buddha test. As anybody knows who has made it to the top, there is only one way to go from there.

Because Kent spent so much time close to the abbot, he was subject to intense teaching on a daily basis. The master pushed him and tested him relentlessly. Lunch hour was often hell because the master was fond of talking while lunch was being served. Shifu would blow up at Kent, turn on him. Or perhaps he would go into a pout. He often expanded small incidents into major catastrophes. He'd withdraw favor, causing Kent to sulk, to be temporarily hurt, left wondering what he had or hadn't done. To be able to stand that kind of heat required really deep roots, for the abbot could really hand it out; he seemed to possess an inexhaustible storehouse of energy. Being near him was a priceless opportunity, but one had to learn to transcend.

Together in joy and sorrow, heaven and hell, my fellow cultivators and I passed our days at Gold Mountain. Unless we were holding a special session, our schedule was similar to that of the Buddhist Lecture Hall. We awakened each morning at 3:40 A.M. to the sound of hardwood boards. It was always cold. We were cultivators—we didn't need heat. (And even if we wanted it, which we didn't, there wasn't any.) We weren't that cold anyway, because we were all bundled up in thick gray robes donated by the Chinese faithful. At 4:00 A.M. we recited mantras and sutras for the better part of an hour, and then conducted two one-hour sits, back to back with a twenty-minute run in between. Nobody did the whole run, as this was a time to whisk into the kitchen and brew tea. At 7:30 A.M. one of the Americans held a sutra review, a discussion of the abbot's previous evening lecture. Then it was open work period until lunch. Most of the people worked on translations during this period. The nuns worked at long fold-up tables with their correctable Selectrics. They'd scrunch their legs into full lotus and, using earphones and reel-to-reel tape recorders, methodically type all of Shifu's words into manuscripts for later editing by joint committees of monastic and lay scholars, who would eventually turn them into books.

Lunch, despite the abbot's counsel to remain unattached, was always the main event each day. Afterward, at 12:30, we filed back into the buddha hall, and for the next hour and a half performed the Great Compassion Repentance Ceremony. The afternoon brought another work period, more meditation, and at 4:30 a language class—usually Chinese or Sanskrit. Then, before evening services and the abbot's formal lecture, we'd have a peaceful hour of meditation to unwind from the day. Following the master's lecture there was another half hour of repentance ceremonies, and then it was lights out.

As for the master, sometimes he rode the public transit buses, but most of the time a lucky disciple got to drive him to the temple. He stayed at a simple house out in the Sunset District a few blocks from the ocean. It was a clean, bare stucco like all the rest. On the ground level was a basement with a garage door leading out into the street. On the mornings I got to pick him up, I usually found him down there working on plaster-of-paris buddhas, little fellows about a foot and a half tall that would eventually end up at our future home, the City of Ten Thousand Buddhas. I'd deliver a dozen bags of plaster, and when the car was emptied out, I'd fill it with finished buddhas. It was a buddha factory!

"My job is creating buddha images," the master said to me one of these mornings. "Living ones!" He smiled at me. "And right now I'm carving you—a little here, a little there."

I'd drop the master outside Gold Mountain around nine or ten, and then go look for a place to park. The master let himself in through a side door to which only he had the key. He made no effort to hide his arrival—he simply didn't choose to use the front door. Sitting in meditation in the buddha hall, we all listened intently as he fumbled with the door, rattled his keys, and cleared his throat.

The master proceeded to the buddha hall first, to his own cushion in the center, and bowed very slowly and softly to the buddhas. After bowing, he would walk over to the foyer where a monk usually sat guarding the door. The monk would then inform him of everything that had happened since the master was last at the monastery. The report included names of anyone who had visited or called, what they wanted, who was in the monastery, who had gone out, and so forth. Then the master slowly walked through the building, carrying under his arm a little bag and a fresh copy of the *Chinese Times*. If people were meditating, he walked around the perimeter of the room, passing inches away from each person. Sometimes he would stop in front of people, sometimes even me, and it made me feel wonderful, exhilarated all over.

Or, if I was working on a project or something, the master would approach and ask, "What doing?"

I'd start explaining myself: "Oh, Shifu, I'm putting together these Chan benches . . . blah, blah, blah . . ." Maybe I'd feel a little superior. After all, I was a foot taller than he was, and I couldn't help but look down on him. And I was an American, and we were brought up thinking we were smarter than the Chinese. But as I rambled on, it became embarrassingly apparent that everything I said involved an "I." Through it all, the master just stood smiling at me from the depths of his unmoving wisdom, acting as if stupid, nodding in agreement, and listening deeply as if it were all new to him. Pretty soon I could hear my voice wax paper thin, I'd hear my own falseness ringing in my ears, and the master would say, "I see, I see!" And I would feel joy and love and perhaps a few more umpteen million kalpas of karma melting away.

Leaving the buddha hall, the master walked up two flights of red-enamel stairs to his room. I can see him now, passing through the rays of sun shining through the two little windows in the buddha hall, dust motes rising slowly in the sunlight, and Shifu among them. He kept a locked room on the top floor. Every morning he unlocked his room and placed the door slightly ajar, indicating he was ready to start his day of service at Gold Mountain. The room was divided in two. The first half served as a receiving parlor for "room-entering" disciples. It was filled with sacred objects—vases, bronze bowls, incense pots, and treasured pieces of Buddhist art from China: priceless calligraphy scrolls from the Tang dynasty, original paintings of bodhisattvas with poetry, innumerable statues of buddhas and sages carved in wood, jade, marble, onyx, or cast in brass and bronze. These were donations that the master had brought with him to help establish Buddhism in America. The master's back room was also filled to overflowing with stuff. I peeked in once and it looked to me like a Tang Dynasty Salvation Army store. The master did his meditating somewhere in the back, well out of sight. We thought he might meditate in a big closet.

Not long after the master settled in in the morning, things really started cooking in the monastery, the energy always fresh and exciting. An elderly Chinese lady was always the first to visit, bringing fresh fruit and flowers every day from Chinatown. After cleaning, organizing, and lighting fresh incense at the various altars, she would then go up to the master's room with a big pot of tea. The master received visitors until well after lunch. Those who wanted to talk with him stood at his door and knocked.

"Who's?" was always the master's reply.

After identifying themselves he'd either invite them in or meet with them in the outer room, and they'd talk about whatever personal problem they had or about the business of running a monastery, translating sutras, and so forth. It was a most exciting thing to visit with the master for any reason. Some of the disciples sought out the master daily with their burdens. As long as they were willing to take the teachings, Shifu was willing to dish them out. Some learned fast. Perhaps the master only needed to point out a problem once or twice, but it might take the disciple the rest of his or her life to get things straightened out. The master understood well that some Dharma seeds would come to fruition much later.

I kept my contact with the master to a minimum. When I did decide to see him, it would only be after things had been building up inside for a long time, until I was virtually bursting with the need to talk. I saw him formally about once a month. Heart pounding wildly, I'd muster up my guts and go knock on his door. He liked to talk to me out in his reception room, where he sat in full lotus on an ancient red-lacquer chair. I would slowly lay out my bowing cloth, bow three and a half respectful bows, and then tell him my problems.

The master was deep and mysterious to me, even though to others he probably appeared quite normal. There were times when I saw him walking in the city, wearing simple, natural fabric—peasant clothing in soft earth tones. He looked like an ordinary Chinese person, someone who only wanted to mind his own business. The ancients say, however, that great wisdom looks like great stupidity. And even Americans say, "Appearances can be deceiving."

The master did everything in his power to teach us how to wake up, to "open enlightenment." Yet he swore he didn't teach us anything. Most of all, he wanted us to be unmoving in our centers. "Bring on the naked ladies!" he once said, in reference to his power of not being moved by external objects. "You know you've arrived," he told us, "when you are able to see that in the midst of problems there really are no problems." He showed us that we could be totally involved in something, and yet at the same time be utterly detached. When normal people act, he told us, they relate everything to this false idea of themselves—"I do this, I think that, I am depressed, I am sick. Yes! I have problems." He paused. "I don't indulge in those kind of thoughts. Why? Actually, I died some time ago," he said. "I didn't die completely, because there was still some trace of desire, but now even that is gone. My ego has no place to live anymore. I don't even know what this body is still doing here. It would be nice to get rid of it, but there's a lot of pressure from my disciples for me to stick around."

It wasn't easy for the master to teach us. Sometimes he threatened to leave—or die—and then we'd straighten up for a while. Once he actually did leave. He flew to Brazil with only a backpack, and he said it was because we weren't following the rules. While he was gone, Babbling Brook was in charge, and there was plenty of oppression, depression, doubts, and fighting—it was affliction city. The whole time he was gone many of us felt guilty and ashamed of our sins—at least I did—and we all knew he was watching us from afar.

Still, we all worked very hard, and most of us were experiencing states we'd never had before. Some people, while rapt in deep meditation, could smell fragrant aromas, as if the whole buddha hall were sprouting lotus flowers. Others had mystical visions, seeing apparitions of Avalokiteshvara Bodhisattva, Amitabha Buddha, or the master. Ralph said that he was able to read my mind when I was sitting next to him—he could hear the *Great Compassion Mantra* rattling around in my brain. I once heard heavenly music during an intensive seven-day Avalokiteshvara session. We'd been reciting the *Great Compassion Mantra* for three days, and as we made our turn around the great hall, I heard a chorus coming down from the rafters as if the place were filled with angels.

I was having experiences right and left, none of them really important, I suppose, but they seemed fantastic. I'd see a bird or a tree in a way I'd never seen one before. Time would sometimes stand still. Every once in a while I'd perceive people as talking meatbags, and they would look so funny: a bag of meat standing there trying to make intelligent conversation. The cobwebs were finally clearing out from my system.

I was actually becoming a real monk now, sitting ever closer to the front altar, right up there with the big boys. Practices I once considered awesome and frightening, I was now doing with the best of them. In the morning, after hot Chinese tea and fifteen minutes of tai chi, I'd gather up my robes on the bench and sit bolt upright like a bell. I could handle full lotus for the full hour! Every morning I stared down along the length of my nose at the patterns in the green linoleum, spacing out even as the wooden fish clicked three times, signaling the beginning of a full hour of sitting. If I used true effort, and didn't waste the time daydreaming, my thoughts would settle down, and the blood and energy that was locked out by the legs in lotus would rush into my head, catalyzing the entrance into some kind of altered state. I'd feel extremely aware. Shifu instructed me to look into the question of who was being aware. I never found anyone. As the clock ticked away, the power circulated and increased. Eventually I'd lose the idea of being in a body, as all systems reached equilibrium. Parts of my body would disappear, one by one, from the head down, until the whole thing was gone, and there was just awareness. It was like the centering of a pot on a wheel, when motion seems to stop—I was cognizant of a total lack of problems. Neither cold, hungry, nor tired, I was like a flower, perfect, complete, in harmony with the universe.

One morning while sitting in meditation, I caught a glimpse of eternity. I just looked up and it was there—it was happening. I thought I'd attained the unattainable, known the unknowable. The brilliant world of endless dust motes in front of my very nose was nirvana, fusing with everything. Thus, thus, eternity, truth.

Everything was simultaneously bursting with life and death, and it didn't matter, because it was all the same. Nothing could be more profound or simple. This was the most important observation of the world I'd ever made. It confirmed my beliefs about Buddhism and rewarded me for my efforts. I just wanted to hug someone and tell them that everything was all right. As if to acknowledge what I was going through, the master walked through the room and stopped in front of me. I couldn't say anything; my river of words had long since run dry. I just sat there, and for a moment he just stood there, too. I was choked up but endlessly alert and alive. I felt so high I could burst apart into a million pieces.

I was not prepared to live in this state, though. It was beyond my control. I had too many obstacles, too much false thinking, and it slipped away.

10. THREE STEPS, ONE BOW

One day, an unusual opportunity arose, and even now I am not sure exactly how it happened. I was in the buddha hall cleaning, and the tall, not-speaking-to-men-at-the-time nun was there, too, arranging something on the other side of the hall. When Shifu came in, I decided it was the right time to ask him if I could go up to Seattle to visit my folks. He listened attentively to my request, and then said OK, no problem. I told him I wasn't sure how I was going to get there and wondered if he had any ideas. As I asked this question, he was walking next to the sitting benches, heading for the red staircase in the back. Laughing, he put his palms together, and imitating a monk bowing every three steps, he said, "Why don't you bow home, just like the sages of old?"

Perhaps he was kidding—I'll never know. Sometimes, it seemed, he presented serious Dharma as a joke. That way, one could take it or leave it without losing face. But it seemed to me that this was a legitimate challenge. The outrageous Dharma seed was planted, and for the next couple of days my mind raced on about the possibilities. What if I were to actually do this? Hell, outrageous was nothing new to me. I'd been outrageously bad most of my life, and it seemed to come naturally. Why not try to be outrageously good?

Shifu had already told us all about the travels of the elder Master Hsu Yun, or Empty Cloud, who made a three-thousand-mile walking pilgrimage across China at the turn of the century, bowing his head to the ground after every third step. During this journey he encountered incredible hardships—suffering from hunger, thirst, and cold—but he never gave up. Eventually, he attained a state of mind that can only be described as "single-minded," bringing to a halt all of his thinking processes. His pilgrimage also had a very profound effect on the people he encountered.

I started to think that maybe this was it; maybe this was a "test to see what I would do." Maybe if I accepted this challenge I'd get enlightened.

The idea began to grow and develop in my mind. Most important to me was the chance this would give me to exclusively cultivate the Dharma. While I bowed along the road praying for world peace with my outer body, I could simultaneously practice the six perfections of a bodhisattva: giving, morality, patience, vigor, concentration, and wisdom. Plus, I had always thrived on adventure, and I was certainly ready for change. This would bring me out of the monastery and onto the road—free! The more I thought about it, the more determined I became to make it happen. Empty Cloud bowed three thousand miles across China; surely I could bow the mere thousand miles up to Seattle. Deep in my heart I decided to go for it.

I didn't tell anyone about my decision. I didn't even inform the master. One cold night in October 1973, after everyone was asleep, I packed up a cloth sack with books, food, and clothing, offered incense to the buddhas, and snuck out onto the gum-laden sidewalks of San Francisco's Mission District. With the monastic door locked firmly behind me, I took three long strides, tossed the bag ahead, then stretched down on my hands and knees and lowered my forehead to the pavement. It was still dark, and the streets were empty. The cement was cold and hard. I felt very strange. The bag, which weighed about thirty pounds, promised to be a big problem. Oh well. I kept going.

The bowing was invigorating exercise! I could feel good things happening to my spine. I bowed steadily in order to get in as much mileage and experience as possible before daybreak. As I shuffled along, I quickly got the physical work figured out, but my mind was racing with conflicting emotions. *I've done a lot of weird, hard-to-explain things in my life*, I thought to myself, *but this is going to take the cake.* Humping along, I headed in the general direction of the Golden Gate Bridge. Daybreak found me in the heart of the Tenderloin. As the city sprang to life all around me, I began to feel the presence of the San Francisco police, who'd been shadowing me for several blocks. I wondered what they were thinking.

By noon I reached the top of Russian Hill. Countless people had watched me, but nobody stopped to talk—they mostly just stared with their mouths open. A rich-looking woman drove by in a white Chrysler. She was in the middle of an intersection when she slammed on the brakes and locked up all her tires. She pulled at her hair and screamed, "Oh my god! Oh my god!" I tried to keep my mind centered as best I could and, ignoring the occasional pangs of embarrassment, kept pounding the pavement. Somewhere deep down inside, beneath all the mixed-up feelings and scattered thoughts, there was serenity, I swear, and even a faint flicker of laughter.

It was time for lunch. Many of the patriarchs and ancients, I'd been told, lived in the wilderness and survived on nothing but wild herbs and pine nuts. I decided to give it a try. I plucked some weeds that were poking up from a crack in the sidewalk. What could be the big difference between these and the greens that went into the average salad? Taking a big handful of grass, I tried to chew and swallow my meal, but it tasted horrible, and I spit it out onto the street. Oh well: I kept going. I bowed down Russian Hill, and by late afternoon found myself in Presidio Park, close to the entrance to Golden Gate Bridge. I had bowed five miles!

I was quite exhausted, so I found a tree to lean against and immediately fell asleep. I awoke several hours later feeling not at all like the same person I had been earlier in the day.

My body was wasted, drained of energy, and I was filled with an empty, silent terror. I had felt this terror before, usually after a long drinking binge, but never so intense. I couldn't go on like this. I looked out at the little lake in front of me, its swimming geese and beautiful surrounding shrubbery, and at the happy couples strolling hand in hand along the shore. Wow! Thirty years old, and look how far I'd strayed from mainstream reality. How did I get so estranged from ordinary life? As I sat in despair, still dressed in my robes and with a freshly shaven head, I contemplated my adult life. So far it was six years in a submarine and two years of drifting as a hippie, the whole thing punctuated by wild drinking episodes. With a stroke of luck I'd run across this little Chinese temple in San Francisco where the teachings of the Buddha were being transmitted. I had found a cave of precious treasures—that cave was my mind, and the treasure was the multifaceted Dharma. Most important, I had found a real teacher, a venerable bhikshu in the patriarchal succession of Chan masters. And now, after finally getting a solid place to cultivate in a secure monastery, I had to go out on the road and make a fool of myself. I'd already left my family, my job, my friends—everything—and here I was leaving the monastery and my teacher to go out and perform this strange form of cultivation. What an escape artist! I was trying to escape from my escaping. I picked up my bag, tossed it over my shoulder, and dragged my defeated and weary bones back to the monastery.

Basking in the relative comforts of Gold Mountain, I slipped back into the routine, and nobody even noticed I had gone. I tried to work up an interest in the activities at the temple, but my heart just wasn't in it. I kept thinking about that one exhilarating day of bowing. Despite all my false thinking and doubts, I had still gone a very real five miles. And there was something wonderful about the experience, something impossible to describe but that had to do with getting past false thinking and reaching to the core.

After a few days of mulling it over, I decided to take another stab at the bowing. This time, however, I revealed my aspirations to the master and requested his opinion and help. The master was immediately interested in and delighted with my idea. He offered every encouragement. And why not? He was the one who had given me the idea. All the ancients agreed that the best way to understand the Dharma is to cultivate difficult practices. "To do what no one else can do, to be patient when no one can be patient—this is what it's all about!" The master recommended that I wait two weeks and start on October 16. Then one evening at the sutra lecture he announced my intentions. A hush fell over the Great Assembly. Suddenly, I was in my glory. I was finally getting the attention I thought I deserved.

"Heng Ju is going to bow a thousand miles for the cause of world peace," the master proclaimed from the high seat, using my ordination name. He declared it with such ease and authority that it seemed like he was guaranteeing a success. From that point onward, I entered into a very fine state of mind, and everyone else seemed to be excited by the idea, too. I received all kinds of encouragement, as well as offers of food, clothing, and camping equipment. Best of all, my buddy Irving (who had taken the name Heng Yo when he ordained), offered to come along and carry the supplies.

The following excerpts are from our journal during the trip; it is a record of our daily thoughts and actions while bowing for world peace.

16 October 1973: The Very Beginning

This morning all the folks at Gold Mountain Monastery, about twenty people altogether, drove us down to the little park by the Golden Gate Bridge where I had previously given up. We didn't waste any time; I started bowing northward, and Heng Yo followed behind with a backpack full of supplies. The monks, nuns, and laypeople recited the 415-syllable *Great Compassion Mantra* while circling around us.

After bowing two blocks, I was preparing to cross the big highway in front of the Marina when a bunch of firetrucks arrived and stopped right in front of us. There was general confusion for a while: we didn't know what they were doing, and they were wondering what we were doing. The street was too busy to cross in the bowing fashion, so I just stood there and bowed in place for a while, thinking about what to do. It must have been quite a spectacle. Finally I decided to simply walk across, and I resumed bowing once I reached the other side.

As we approached the long entrance-ramp to the bridge, the trucks departed, and Heng Yo and I were on our own. Heng Yo would go up ahead a few hundred feet with the equipment, and then bow in place until I passed him by; then he would pick up the gear and go bow up ahead some more.

At the Golden Gate Bridge, we met our first obstacle. A bridge official came running out and said that if we were going to do "that" across his bridge, he was going to bust us. He said that we could "either walk across like normal human beings or not go at all." Then he said, "So, what is it? What are you going to do?" We could see that he was looking for trouble. I said, "We're going to think about it for a while," which flustered him, but there was nothing he could say about that. We bowed in place for a while, and then decided that there was no choice but to walk across like "normal human beings." On the other side, in Marin County, we continued bowing, and I suddenly remembered the master's departing words: "Tomorrow Heng Ju and Heng Yo will cross the Golden Gate Bridge in a single thought."

From here, we plan to head on through Stinson Beach and all the way up Highway 1 to its end in Legget, California. From there we will take Highway 101 all the way up to the middle of Washington State, and then we'll head inland to Seattle.

30 October 1973

Now, as the thin, snaking highway begins its descent back to the coast, we have met with disaster.

We were just a mile short of the coastal town of Bodega Bay when I felt the call to go to the bathroom. Needless to say, there were no bathrooms, so I crawled off the highway into a little clump of bushes to perform my daily duty. Unfortunately, there wasn't any toilet paper available, so I grabbed at the nearest bush and pulled off a handful of bright orange leaves. That was a costly mistake! I soon found out that those pretty little gems were, in fact, poison oak. (I had always thought poison oak was green.) Thinking didn't help at this point. We stopped bowing, and by evening my entire body was itching something terrible. It kept me up all night; I didn't get a moment's sleep. I did, however, remember to recite the name of Avalokiteshvara Bodhisattva, and it helped keep my mind off the pain.

By morning, I could hardly move, much less bow, so Heng Yo and I just sat down on a mound of dirt by the side of the road. We were both in total wretchedness. Once again, I was overwhelmed with doubts and with the sense of impossibility and unreality of what we were doing. Here we were, with half of California, all of Oregon, and all of Washington left to bow through, and I didn't even know how to wipe my ass!

We sat there for several hours. We couldn't turn back—or could we? We definitely couldn't go on, so we sat and watched the cars pass by. There seemed to be no conceivable way to solve our problem. Suddenly, though, as if in magical response to our dilemma, two familiar-looking vans pulled to a stop before us. Out popped the whole group from Gold Mountain! And the master, too! We moved to an empty parking lot in front of an abandoned cannery. They brought out food, clothing, medicine, everything that we needed, even toilet paper. What a wonderful feeling in the air.

We all sat down in a circle, about fifteen feet in diameter. First, Heng Yo and I explained our experiences over the last few days; then one by one the monks and nuns gave short Dharma talks. While they spoke, the master took my right hand and began rubbing it. He rubbed and rubbed, very softly, while he recited a mantra. Gradually, I could feel every bit of tension and pain leave my body. I couldn't hear what anyone was saying; I could only feel the warmth of the afternoon sun. Nothing else mattered.

Just before they left, I asked the master, "Last night I called for Avalokiteshvara Bodhisattva to come and rescue me, and today you and the people of Gold Mountain have come to the rescue. Isn't this quite a coincidence?"

The master immediately replied, "It's no big thing. Any time you like, just give a call. I'll be there."

I learned a lot today. For one thing, I'll never forget what poison oak looks like as long as I live, and I'll do my best to save others from this painful experience. But more important, I got a better understanding of what I call the master's central philosophy: "Everything's OK." Those two words are the essence of his teaching; I have heard them spoken hundreds of times. "Everything's OK" doesn't mean that you can just run out and do whatever you please. No, "Everything's OK" is a very disciplined state of mind, wherein one observes the rise and fall of all conditioned things with complete detachment. It is a place of no-place. And yet, without leaving this detachment, one can be totally involved and live a responsible and mature life. It is something that can be sought after and obtained. No matter how bad conditions may seem in the world of phenomena, ultimately everything's OK.

12 November 1973

This highway has been cut through rocky, volcanic cliffs that jut straight up hundreds of feet above the beach. The view is awesome here, and so is the weather. Gale-force winds blow in from the sea, and of course the rain keeps us soaked to the bone.

Just for a pleasant diversion, we made a side trip today. One of our sangha members, Gwo Mien, had mentioned before we left that we would be welcome at a small Native American reservation about four miles inland. So early in the afternoon, we secured the bowing supplies, walked into Stewarts Point, bought a few supplies at the general store, and then proceeded inland on a little winding road. Darkness quickly fell, and a ferocious rain came pouring down. It became pitch black, the heavy cloud banks totally obscuring the moonlight. It got to the point where we actually couldn't even see our own hands, much less the road. The rain was hammering at us like millions of watery bullets. We stumbled up the mountain, with a raging creek to our left and a steep precipice on the right. I was walking in front, and Heng Yo was following, when I realized that he was no longer with me. "Heng Yo!" I cried out. No answer. Fear swelled inside me. "Yo, where are you?" The only sound was the relentless rain and the raging creek.

Finally, I heard his voice, and we began yelling at each other until we could trace the sound out and find each other. I never did see him; I ran into him. He said that he had fallen off the road into the canyon and had never been so scared in his life, rolling down, down a mountain, blind. Foolishly, we had left our flashlight back at the bowing spot, but we did have a little piece of rope with us. We fumbled around and finally tied ourselves together with a ten-foot space between us. Then we continued the ascent. I went first, gingerly feeling each step of the way by scraping my boot on the road ahead, while Heng Yo followed behind, ready to stop me should I fall over the side. We proceeded like this for a couple of hours—cold, wet, and lost on our own planet. We had gone too far to turn back; our only hope was to go on. We were seriously wondering if we were going to live through this little trip.

It was some time after midnight when we stopped walking, broke out a nylon tarp, and huddled together under it in the middle of the road. We were shivering and wet, but we managed to light a candle and break out the map to see where we were. The way it looked, we had another mile to go. It would take all night at this rate. Suddenly we saw a flicker of light from down the mountain. A vehicle was coming: it was an old Native American in a truck. He picked us up and gave us a ride to the reservation. But when we inquired there, we were told that white men were not allowed.

We were too cold and wet to do anything else but turn around and keep moving. We headed down the mountain, and it was hell for a while, but then the moon began to shine through the clouds, and we made it back to Stewarts Point just before sunrise. We found an abandoned motel to sneak into, and despite the fact that there was a dead cat rotting away on one of the armchairs, it was like the Hilton to us.

4 December 1973

It was a big day today as we bowed through the city of Fort Bragg. Bus drivers, students, kids, old folks, hippies, young girls—all came out to see us. Some drunken motorcyclists stopped their big Triumphs and Harleys and began to hassle us, but today I felt really strong and didn't want to stop for anything, so I passed them off to Heng Yo. They pestered him for a while, asking him why the hell we were doing what we were doing. He asked them why the hell they were doing what *they* were doing, and that finally shut them up. In the heart of town, a Catholic priest walked up to me and said in a mournful voice, "Where are you going in such a slow and painful manner?" I tried to explain our trip, but I could see that he was only feeling sorry for me. After he left, I got to thinking about it. Actually there is no pain at all. He's just projecting it. It is quite invigorating work in reality. Never before have I been in such good physical shape! The painfulness is his, not mine!

I'm really delighted by these encounters. Sometimes I don't recognize what's happening at first, but usually after a little more bowing and reflection they become clear. I realize what I said that was right and what I should have said, and I store all this information for the next encounter. It's a way to learn the Dharma of the "eight winds."

The eight winds are gain and loss, ridicule and flattery, praise and blame, and joy and sorrow. We all have these winds constantly blowing against us. The idea is to practice stillness in the face of them. For example, there are many people who praise our work and refer to us as holy men, sages, and so on. Others call us neurotic, idol-worshipping heathens. Moved by the former, we become more egotistical. Moved by the latter, we become sad and depressed. Therefore we are learning to view all talk as so many empty words, and merely continue on our "slow and painful" way.

Now we're camped behind a slow and painful bulldozer in a gravel company lot just north of the city.

8 January 1974

Garberville: The new year has begun and the trip is off to a fresh start. It feels totally exhilarating being out here. It seems as if we have encountered and linked up with some awesome kind of spiritual power that keeps multiplying. We are a mere part of it. It comes from the master, it comes from within us, it comes from the people we meet. More and more I am beginning to appreciate the truth of the master's statement, "You must learn to turn the world, and not be turned by it." Who knows what wonders or hardships lie ahead? I feel ready to meet them with a level and equal mind. We have now traveled over 200 miles, and have 135 miles to go, as the crow flies, to the Oregon line.

13 January 1974

Passing through Myers Flat, I had an encounter with a man in a fire-engine-red pickup truck. He was parked outside of town waiting; there was no one around except me and him. Heng Yo was at the laundromat, drying out the gear. As I passed near his truck, he started yelling at me. He was drunk and really angry. "What the hell are you trying to prove? What do you think you are doing?" he yelled over a public-address system mounted on the top of his cab. I wasn't sure how to respond to him, so I just kept bowing. He began driving right alongside of me, sparing no words, cursing and shouting obscenities. He was truly a fireman with much fire.

This weird scene continued for several minutes, during which time I still hadn't said a word. Finally, after thoroughly emptying himself of his rage, he began to break down and cry. "Why won't you talk to me?" he wailed. "What kind of religion is this that won't permit you to talk to me?"

I stopped bowing and finally spoke. "I am not doing any harm. Why are you upset?"

"Why can't you pray alone?" he said.

"I've prayed alone for several years," I said. "I need some fresh air."

"Look," he said, "why can't you do good, like me? I'm a fireman; I save people's lives. Now that has a real use. Listen, I'm sorry that I got mad, but there's a lot of mean loggers up north of here, and they're not going to like this bowing-along-the-road business."

"Well," I said, "I'm sorry also, but this is what I do; it's very meaningful to me. I'm sorry I upset you."

"Well," he said, "I been drinking, and I get angry real easy. Lesh forget the whole thing, OK?"

"OK."

5 February 1974

Since it is such a nasty day out, we didn't leave Patrick's Point State Park today. We spent most of the day reading, meditating, walking along the cliffs, and relaxing. At sunset we gave each other a Dharma talk and drilled each other on Chinese vocabulary. I have a pocket Chinese dictionary I have been using to drill Heng Yo during rest periods. His Chinese is excellent. In fact Heng Yo is a remarkable person in many ways. Vigorous, industrious, enthusiastic, meticulous, responsible, intelligent, and sensitive: that's what he is. Whether installing plumbing, developing film, translating scriptures, baking bread, sitting in full lotus, or setting up the five-pound tent on a rocky cliff, he does it clearly and precisely, as if he were being well paid for it. He concentrates on the work before him and gets it done.

Now of course it wouldn't be a fair appraisal if I just mentioned his good points, so I must add, and mind you this is not a big fault, that he does at times take things a little too personally. He can upon occasion fall into a state that I call the Deep Pisces Blues, and more often than not he manages to pull me into it also. When he gets "that" look on his face, I know that somewhere, somehow, I have done something wrong.

At that point, it's up to me to figure out what I did wrong, and reconcile the differences. Often I say, "Hey, Yo! Let's stop for a while and have some hot chocolate." The Hot Chocolate Dharma has solved more problems on this trip for both of us than any other method we could think of. Usually I find that I, in fact, actually was inconsiderate in some form or another, and when the roots of the incident are dug up, Heng Yo returns to being his cheerful, vigorous self. And I return to being my sometimes-obnoxious self, and we're off down the road.

6 February 1974

We made five miles and are now camped right on a sandy beach. We have a roaring bonfire going. Today we passed Big Lagoon County Park. It was a strange passage. As I bowed alongside the lagoon I began to lose my sense of time and distance. There was a heavy wind with lots of mist blowing in from the sea. I experienced the sensation that I was standing in one place bowing, absolutely still while all the world was moving past me. Perhaps it wasn't so much an exalted state of consciousness as it was the optics of the situation. The immense vastness of the scene and the long narrow highway disappearing like an endless thread over the horizon helped create the effect. In any case I must have set some kind of record for myself as I bowed over a mile and a quarter without once breaking pace. The energy just kept coming, and it felt good.

22 February 1974

We bowed along the ridge of a large hill, in the midst of Jedediah Smith Redwoods State Park. Tomorrow or the next day we will begin our descent into Crescent City, the last major town in California. The weather was most strange today. We encountered snow, rain, hail, and a brilliant sun, all within the same hour.

Toward day's end, a car stopped, and a long-haired man got out and came running toward me, yelling, "Tim! Tim!" It was Dane from the Family Farm, the old commune in Washington. He was quite surprised to see me bowing but quickly recovered and invited us to stop at his house for pancakes when we pass by.

23 February 1974

There was a lot of action as we made our passage through Crescent City today. Three ladies, Mrs. Extine, Mrs. Crites, and Mrs. Ross, brought us presents. Heng Yo and I decided to open a bank account and use the money people offer us for the construction of a new monastery.

While in Arcata, we picked up a transistor radio for twenty-five cents at a thrift store. All it needed was a new battery. Since then, every night after meditation we have been listening to the news and weather reports. As we approached Crescent City this morning, Heng Yo tuned in and heard Bill Stamps of Radio KPOD giving a step-by-step account of our progress. Bill is a real bright personality who takes pride in keeping his audience well informed. He sounds something like this: "Well, the last time I saw them two monks, they were bowing along the oceanfront getting ready to make the turn into town. If any of you all have seen them, call me and let me know where they are. Yes, folks, this is really something! You should see that big Heng Ju move out! He's about six and a half feet tall, and when he takes a step he covers about seven feet of ground! This is really quite the undertaking! And his friend Heng Joe, or is it Hang Hoe? Well in any case, whatever his name is, the shorter one is always right there with the cart. What a fine guy he is! I tell you folks, I've never seen anything like it. Let's all of us try to show these two boys that Crescent City really appreciates what they are doing!"

I kept fairly close to Heng Yo as we went through the city, and we both listened to the little radio, which was taped to the outside of the cart. Bill *was* well informed. He talked a lot about various aspects of Buddhism, and he even knew about Master Hsu Yun's trip across China. In the afternoon Bill himself appeared with a portable recorder and taped an interview with us. He looked like an overgrown leprechaun with his pointed shoes, plaid pants, red blazer, fuzzy beard, and devilish eyes.

At the end of town, we met Mr. Long, the city's only blacksmith. He did a good deal of free welding on the buggy. Last of all, we met Howard Cronk, owner of the Totem Hotel, who gave us a room for the night.

29 March 1974

This morning was one of those times when affliction and bitterness was in the air and it seemed as if nothing could make them go away. I was mad at Heng Yo for some silly reason or another, and I knew that I shouldn't be, but I couldn't seem to get rid of it. I began reciting Avalokiteshvara Bodhisattva's name with real vigor, hoping that somehow this compassionate being who is capable of doing miraculous things would help me out. Having made this thought, I looked up ahead to see an old Chevy panel truck stopping on the side of the road. Two men got out and helped a woman out of the truck. She was blind.

The three of them approached me, and Heng Yo came over too. The woman, who looked like she was in her early thirties, asked if I was the bowing monk that she had heard so much about. "Yes," I said. She held my hand for several minutes, and we all stood there in silence. I could feel my afflictions rapidly dissolving. The sun felt warm and good. After a while she said, "You are a really peaceful person. I can feel it." Then she told us how happy she was that we were doing this thing, and that there were a lot of people with us and thinking about us every step of the way. By the time they left, my afflictions were totally gone.

5 May 1974

Last night we took up the invitation of an ex-Marine and former missionary to China to stay in his home. It was a mistake. Although he and his family were extremely hospitable to us, beneath it all was an intense desire to convert and "save" us. All night long, first in English, then in Chinese, he never let up. He had found everlasting life, and he wasn't going to be happy until we'd found it too. There wasn't any real problem during the evening, but in the morning, when he took us out to the bowing area, a little friction arose. By this time he was concentrating his efforts mostly on Heng Yo; I think he'd pretty much written me off as a lost cause. We had just gotten out of the car on the north end of Reedsport at the Smith River bridge when he said to Yo, "I hope you boys will give up your paganistic idol worshipping and accept the Lord. Especially you, Heng Yo, being a chosen one." Yo quickly replied, "We're all chosen ones." The scene ended with all of us getting upset and yelling at each other, until finally he jumped in his car and roared off. It was too bad, because I know he really meant well.

This morning we found a bag of fresh fruit in our path. On it a note read, "May the longtime sun shine upon you, and all love surround you, and the pure light within you guide your way on," which I think is a quote from a song by the Incredible String Band. In the evening, Deputy Sheriff Richard Knack brought us a gallon of pure water and showed us a good place to set up camp. Now we are sitting beside the tent, simmering beans over a fire for tomorrow's lunch. A warm breeze is coming off the ocean, and a small brook is gurgling away. The moon is full and thousands of stars are out.

17 May 1974

Bowed six and a half miles in the sunshine. This morning, just north of the Newport city limits, I stopped to take a leak in the loos behind a modern-looking Lutheran Church. In passing, I noticed a sign on the church that read "Mr. Olson, Pastor." I didn't think anything of it at the time. Later, I continued bowing northward, and after about two hours, a middle-aged couple stopped to ask me the usual questions. I noticed that they looked pretty bright, so I asked them if they were of any particular religious affiliation.

"Yes," the man replied, "We are both Lutherans."

Now, I have never been in Newport before, and I have no idea what prompted me to say it, but I said right back to him, "Oh, yes; Mr. and Mrs. Olson!" It was a direct hit; they both almost fell over. Of all the Lutherans in Newport it just happened to be them. I kept a straight face and continued talking for a few minutes. They listened to every word!

The petite Mrs. Cude came out to share some of her wealth with us. She gave us a bag of whole wheat bread, cheese, and fruits. Unfortunately, that wasn't all she wanted to share with us; she was intent on giving us a big hug, and we had to use all the skillful means we could muster to fend her off. Two riders on chopped Harley Davidsons talked with me for a few minutes. They seemed to appreciate the idea of being all alone out here on the road.

18 May 1974

A rookie sheriff's deputy stopped and put us in the back of his car. He radioed headquarters to have them check the computer and see if we were criminals. He thought we were either escaped convicts, AWOL sailors, or insane asylum patients. But there wasn't a thing he could bust us for, so he finally let us go.

As we passed through Depoe Bay, a Mrs. Walter met us at the northern city limits and warned us that there was a houseful of drunks waiting for us up ahead. She said that they had been drinking all day and were having a big party waiting for us to come along. Some of them had been throwing beer cans out on the road; others had been making mock prostrations on the shoulder. As we stood there discussing the issue, Mr. Baker, owner of the local motel, came running out and offered us a free room. I looked up ahead about one block and saw the group they were talking about. Every once in a while one of them would dart out on the road to see if we were coming. Yes, this was the age-old choice again: should we accept the milk of human kindness, or should we march off to war? I'd had enough milk for the day; I wanted action.

I told Heng Yo, "Why don't you go back to the motel and start unloading the gear? I'll bow for another hour or so, and then walk back." "Nothing doing!" replied Yo. "I'm going out there, and I'm going out there now!" He reached down, grabbed the pack, threw it over his shoulders, then grabbed the buggy and started huffin' down the road directly toward the drunks.

"Stop! You boys are making a terrible mistake!" One of the ladies yelled. I put on my gloves, adjusted my trusty kneepads, and started performing my ritual down the highway. The words of my mantra rattled through my mind like a freight train. Heng Yo approached the group with unswerving determination. From my vantage point about a hundred feet behind, I could see there were about eleven of them, but they seemed to be pushed away as Heng Yo approached.

In fact it appeared that they were scared. Heng Yo kept trucking straight at them, and by the time he got within fifty feet, they had completely scattered. Most of them headed back to the house. One of them tossed a few pebbles from a safe distance, but his heart wasn't in it. Heng Yo stopped directly in front of the house and waited for me to pass. It was as if a bulldozer had cleared the way: I went by without any problem. Only a few remarks were mouthed, but they had no power to them. We were so energized from the encounter that we bowed another two and a half miles, making it an eight-and-a-half-mile day, our longest so far. Just as we prepared to set up camp off the highway, a carload of people who were at the party came out and apologized. Yo said, "Oh, don't worry about it."

25 May 1974

An old truck with a wooden house on the back stopped, and four shaggy-looking souls came out to greet us. The shaggiest of the group said, "Would you guys like some fresh goat's milk?"

"Yes," I said without delay. At that, he walked over to the back door of the truck, swung it open, and there inside was a real live nanny goat, with her stern section toward us. He reached in under her, procured an empty quart bottle, and proceeded to relieve nanny of just that much of her warm goods. Afterward we stood in a circle and passed the bottle around. "It don't come no fresher," I remarked.

The tallest one, who looked like a transformation-body of Ben-

Hur, said: "Please tell us just exactly what have you learned on this trip." My mind began to whirl as I flashed back on the hundreds of miles and the thousands of people we had already encountered.

What an incredible question to ask! There was no way I could answer it in a few words, so I just remained silent. There was a long pause as we all stood there. Finally the tall one said, "We think what you two are doing is really worth it; we hope you make it!"

4 June 1974

Heavy storm, so we made no progress today. We are camped halfway between hell and nowhere in dripping-wet Oregon. We didn't make a proper drainage ditch last night, so now we are in the process of submerging. There is an ever-growing pool of water in the back section of the tent. Not only that, but I burned a big hole in my foam pad while trying to light the stove with a small splash of fuel. For a few seconds it looked as if the whole tent were going to burn down. Lighting the stove inside the tent should be left only to those brave souls who have already cut off the cycle of birth and death! Then, once the little devil was running, I managed to scorch the oatmeal. Five minutes later I broke the salt shaker, liberating half a cup of salt all over the tent. What a day! We're sinking and bobbing in the sea of our own afflictions.

4 July 1974

My family came out to the bowing area and picked us up. We spent the Independence Day holiday with them at our home in Belfair. My mother took quite a liking to Heng Yo and helped him make a bhikshu shirt on her sewing machine. My dad fixed us up with a backpack and two sleeping bags. Even though it rained the whole time we were there, it was wonderful to be with the folks again.

12 July 1974

Today we bowed through metropolitan Tacoma. Here and there large crowds would gather and ask questions: "What are you doing? Where are you going? What do the three steps signify? Do you take turns pulling the cart? Do you know kung fu? Can we take your picture?" Methodists and Baptists, ministers and laypeople, blacks and whites: all came out to offer their opinions or wish us luck. Mostly the latter. As we approached the thick of the downtown area a woman who must have been in her late sixties came up to Heng Yo and told him that she had come to lead us through town. She said that God had sent her "to guide us through Tacoma." And that's exactly what she did. Not only that, but early in the day a chubby barefoot lad resembling Huckleberry Finn offered his services and, without another word, pulled the buggy all the way through town.

In the late afternoon when we had made it through downtown and were bowing out through the flat industrial harbor area, we experienced a really close call. About a half a block away, I happened to notice a man come out of a tavern with a case of beer under his arm. He got into a red 1960 Pontiac convertible and, spinning his tires, came roaring out of the parking lot. He turned around a corner and came squealing out onto the main road. Then, with his engine racing wildly, he accelerated in our direction. We were standing together on the curb. He was doing about fifty miles an hour as he approached us when suddenly he cranked over on his steering wheel and jumped up onto the curb. He was going to mow us down! It all happened so fast that there wasn't time to think, or move, or anything. We could only stand there and watch it happen. The red streak missed my leg by something like six inches. Then, just as suddenly as he appeared, he was gone.

Once again, I was amazed by my own reactions, and Yo's, too. There was no fear. The event was empty. It was like watching a scene from a television show. There just didn't seem to be anything going on at all. Some people from the tavern came out and asked us if we were all right. We said yes. They had taken up a collection for us and invited us into the tavern to say a few words.

Halfway through the mudflats area, we made camp under a bridge. Windy night, crackling fire, sitting in Chan.

31 July 1974

I thought it would have happened long ago, but finally it has happened. I have developed a large swelling under my left kneecap. I don't know how long we can continue with it—it seems to be getting worse all the time. We made a few miles this morning, but the knee is swelling bigger and looks as if it's getting infected. It's all purple and yellow. I called up my old high school friend Jon Myers. We went into the navy together, and now he is a color television repairman for RCA in the north end of Seattle. He came out here to pick us up and, hearing about my leg, told us we should stay at his home until it is healed. It has been over five years since I've seen Jon.

1–4 August 1974

We spent the last three days at Jon's house. Although I've been soaking the knee every night, the swelling hasn't gone down. In my estimation it looks as if it will take two weeks or more to heal, considering, of course, that no bowing is done on it. In Buddhism, this is known as a karmic obstacle.

5 August 1974

Today we finally decided to seek the master's advice. I called the temple and asked him what the best cure would be. I explained how my knee was swollen, how it would take a long time to heal, and how bowing would only make it worse.

The master did not hesitate in his reply: "Basically, there is no problem. The best cure for your knee is to get out there and finish your bowing."

I was stunned by his answer. If it had been anybody else, I would have argued. But Heng Yo and I packed up the gear, said goodbye to Jon, and got out there on Highway 9 where we had left off. I started bowing, and was surprised to find that there was no pain! I continued bowing and got in four miles before the day was over. The swelling had gone down. It was nothing short of a miracle.

7 August 1974

We have reached Arlington, and the end of the trip is rapidly approaching. Looking at the maps, I remember the doubts and fears that haunted us earlier. They are gone now, and unless something very unusual takes place, it appears that we will make it.

During the first part of the trip I remember the butterflies I used to get at the thought of going out and facing all those people; I felt a need to try to explain myself to everyone. I could see by the disapproving looks on many of their faces that they didn't like either me or what I was doing. Not only the bowing but also the mere appearance of a monk with a shaven head was enough to set off a lot of scowls.

Things have changed quite a bit as we have worked our way north. The news media has played a great part in explaining what's going on. People seem to know us already, having read about us for months preceding our arrival. They treat us like long-lost relatives, and the few that do scowl now we just don't pay any attention to.

15 August 1974

Another one of those hot dusty days. Heavy traffic, logging trucks, and affliction everywhere. We bowed along Highway 20 into the little town of Van Horn. The Olsons, who own the general store and gas station, invited us in for a cool pop. There was a lot of activity around the place; these folks had been hearing about us for months. Kids and dogs were milling around everywhere. At one point, I noticed an old man, short, bearded, and bespectacled, wandering around outside the station. He was talking to the kids, and although I don't think he had ever been there before, he behaved like he was old friends with everyone. He had a white truck with a homemade trailer behind it and two dogs that he was trying to give away. I was taken aback when he walked up to me and asked me if I called myself a Buddhist. I noticed that he was totally relaxed and centered.

"Why, ahh, ahh, yes," I replied, wondering what he was getting at.

"Do you want to hear what the Buddha taught in plain English?" he asked. I didn't want to say no, because that wouldn't be right. And I didn't want to say yes, because that would imply that I didn't already know. I looked around and there was a small crowd gathering. He had a mischievous gleam in his eye.

"What did the Buddha teach?" I finally said.

"The Buddha taught compassion. The Buddha said that we should stop knocking each other around, but most people don't buy it!"

I was sure this little man could see right through me, but I quickly replied, "Buy what?"

"What the Buddha taught!" laughed the little man. "I don't think that you are a complete convert," he said.

Boy, he was really putting me on the spot! "I didn't say I was perfect," I replied. I had shifted totally into my own defense. The little man paused, and then he moved closer and looked right into my eyes. I was beginning to steadily flash on how angry I had been toward Heng Yo during the last few weeks.

"The Buddha taught compassion. Be more compassionate!" he said.

Then he took off his glasses and stuck his face up about twelve inches in front of mine. "I'm not your enemy; I'm your friend. How many people do you know who would talk to you like this?"

By this time I was completely overwhelmed, not to mention embarrassed. I had never seen this guy before, yet he had zeroed right in on my number as if I were transparent. All the people were looking at me. Everything was quiet, and I was absolutely speechless.

I didn't know what to do or say, so I went back out on the road and continued bowing. Only afterward did I begin to realize just how miraculous an encounter it was. Just as the master had often done, this man was talking right through my false front, directly to my attachments. As I bowed along, I began to feel a sense of shame that I hadn't felt in a long time. I really had been mean to Heng Yo in many, many ways. Most of the time it was very indirect and subtle; nevertheless, it was always very irritating. I felt terrible about it. I recalled a verse that the master once wrote:

Truly recognize your own faults,
Don't discuss the faults of others.
Others' faults are just your own.
Being one substance with everyone
Is called the Great Compassion.

I scurried down the highway until I reached the spot where Heng Yo was waiting with the cart. He had missed my encounter with the old man, so I told him what had happened. We sat down and mixed up some lemonade powder with some fresh Skagit River water. I looked at him directly for the first time in a long time. For a short moment, we shared a smile of silent understanding. I felt old, old, old. Then we both got up and continued on.

17 August 1974

Heng Yo writes:

Last night I heard a yell coming out of the sleeping Heng Ju. "Hey, there's monsters under this freeway!" he called out in a loud and clear voice. After he woke up, he told me he had dreamed he was picking up the road, just as if it were a piece of rug, and beneath it were myriad demonic-looking creatures.

We got up early and bowed through the little town of Marblemount before many people were up, and continued three miles to the monastery site without stopping to rest. The excitement was high, and we reached the property at 10:30 A.M. Ju made his final bow. We ended the trip by reciting the *Great Compassion Mantra* several times and transferring any merit we may have acquired to living beings everywhere. Then we had lunch on a big rock bank with the Skagit River flowing rapidly below us.

At the end of the day, we went up to the top of Sauk Mountain, where there is an unbelievably awesome view of the whole Skagit Valley and of the last forty-five miles we had bowed. The sun was just beginning to set as we reached the summit at fifty-five hundred feet. Oceans of pink and blue clouds were rolling in over the delta like giant puffs of cotton candy. We were surrounded by hundreds of giant mountains, all drenched in numberless shades of orange and purple. Mount Baker loomed in front of us as if in deep samadhi. The stars were beginning to appear. Suddenly we noticed a strange light on the horizon. One minute it looked like a crescent, the next minute like a bouncing ball. It appeared and disappeared several times, then suddenly got very bright and shot off like a ball of fire. To the left of it, we noticed a huge black and gray cloud formation perhaps one hundred miles in length, which took the unmistakable form of a fire-breathing dragon. It looked like it was chasing the ball of light.

Then darkness came, and with it, all of the rain that had been storing up for the last few weeks. It broke loose in the biggest torrent we had seen in a long time. I looked up in sheer wonder as the storm blew in. The trip was over.

11. THE FALL

We returned to a hero's welcome at Gold Mountain, with much excitement and fanfare. Now it truly seemed that the Buddhadharma was off to a strong start in the West. Heng Yo and I were treated as if we were the Chan answer to the Beatles.

About this time a winter Chan session started up, and everyone dropped everything and started in on the twenty-one-hours-a-day meditation thing. I managed to sit strongly and circulate the energy for about two weeks. Then one day Shifu interrupted the session and told me, Brother Kent, and Heng Sure, a new monk, that we were going to represent him at Mayor Moscone's gala inaugural celebration.

In the weeks prior to the voting, Gold Mountain had opened its doors and allowed each of the mayoral candidates a chance to get together with our neighbors in informal group discussions about the issues. Most of the candidates took advantage of the offer, and we had some very lively, interesting gatherings. Every night that they came, Shifu would come down and chat with them.

But now I had been exclusively restricting and purifying my senses for the better part of two weeks—not to mention the yearlong bowing pilgrimage before then—and suddenly I was downtown in a crowd of ten thousand. The three of us walking abreast in our robes and with our shaven heads must have been quite a sight. I wasn't the least bit worried about it, however, because I was in a state like I'd never known before. I was walking on clouds, rainbows beneath my arhat shoes. I was filled with power and light and some kind of awesome clairvoyance. People passed me in the halls as if part of a colorful dream. In their mostly sad faces I could see lifetimes of karma. I could read them like a book. Everything was clear, in a nonverbal kind of way. I could see right through them. I mean, I certainly hadn't achieved *anuttarasamyaksambodhi*—the ultimate right and perfect enlightenment—but I was sure getting a nice taste of it. This was obviously what it was all about. This was the way to live on the planet earth! Here I was, without a thing in the world—no job, no wife, no future, no security, no nothing—and I felt like a walking god. I was free from affliction, worry, fear, desire, and filled with existential bliss. What a way to be! The outer world just seemed like one big swirling amorphous mass, all part of our common buddha mind. There was not one problem in the world in the midst of all this horrendous karma of suffering.

My wonderful state, however, could not last. After a day or so back in the world, my senses returned to perpetual overload, and I once again rejoined the ranks of the common man.

The day before we had made it to Marblemount, the end of our journey, the master had called Heng Yo and me and asked if we'd like to accompany him on a Dharma tour to Hong Kong, Taiwan, Singapore, Japan, India, Nepal, Sri Lanka, and Vietnam. We'd be giving talks and visiting some of the places where the Buddha lived.

"Traveling with me is a lot of suffering," the master had warned when he first extended the invitation. "Are you sure you want to go?" Of course I was sure.

Apparently Buddhists abroad had heard about our bowing trip and wanted to see us in person. Heads still reeling from all the fame and attention, Yo and I booked tickets and secured our visas. The next thing we knew we were on the plane winging it to the Far East with an enlightened Chan master as our traveling companion.

In Hong Kong, we stayed at the master's old temple, the Buddhist Lecture Hall. It was basically just a room on the eleventh floor of a building next to the Happy Valley race track. It was here where we began our lecture series. Heng Yo and I, sitting on either side of the master, talked for ten minutes each, and then the master would give a talk for about forty minutes.

We stayed at the Buddhist Lecture Hall for a couple of days, and the whole time, Shifu was surrounded by two dozen of the most spiritually beautiful Cantonese lay ladies one could ever see. These women were utterly and unconditionally devoted to the master. It was as though they had one mind, like a swarm of bees or a flock of birds. The master spoke to them in Mandarin and they spoke to him in Cantonese. This went on for hours every day. Sometimes he would yell and scream, and they would all spread out and flatten against the walls as if being blown by a big hurricane. Other times he would speak softly and they would gather at his feet like children. It was something to see. These were some of his most loyal disciples, part of the core group that helped get him going in America.

It was at the Buddhist Lecture Hall that I began to notice something different about my relationship with the master. All during the bowing trip he had been praising me and encouraging me, and I had basked in the fame and glory like a newborn babe taking his mother's milk. Now he seemed neither for nor against me. He was just kind of leaving me alone. It was fine, I told myself; it was no big deal.

Heng Yo, however, was under full attack. It started the day we arrived in Hong Kong. It was a Sunday, and Yo was supposed to call the airline ticketing agency and check up on our flight. He called, but no one answered.

"I thought I told you to call about the airplane?" Shifu screamed at him.

"I did call the airlines, Shifu," Heng Yo replied. "But it's Sunday, and they're not working today. No one answered."

"I don't believe you!" Shifu yelled.

"No, it's true, master. I called them twice."

"I still don't believe you!" shouted the master. Yo's face dropped and hung toward the ground like an sad moon.

"OK, Shifu. I'll call them again if you like." Yo got on the phone and called, but no one answered.

"I called them, Shifu, but no one answered."

"I still don't believe you. What do I have to do, call them myself?"

Yo got on the phone again and let it ring and ring. Finally someone answered it, and he was able to attend to our schedule.

From Hong Kong we flew to India. When the plane touched down in Calcutta the smoke from all the burning cow dung was overpowering—enough to make the eyes water. Shifu's comment on landing was a mix of English and Chinese: "Jeiga difong jen shr terrible." ("This place is certainly terrible.") I couldn't believe it myself. The optics were so different it felt like we had landed on another planet. All along the sidewalks of the city I saw the homeless sleeping, clothed only in rag robes. Poverty and misery prevailed.

Everywhere we traveled beggars accosted us. At the place of Buddha's enlightenment, an old beggar woman approached us and stuck her begging bowl out at the master and started yelling, "Uh! Uh! Uh!" in a very mean and demanding way. I will never forget what followed as long as I live. Shifu grabbed the extended bowl and started yelling, "Uh! Uh! Uh!" back at her. The woman was confounded, but she started tugging back, and the two of them just stood there tugging and going "Uh! Uh! Uh!" What is the meaning of this? Well, I never said I could interpret everything the master did.

After India, we traveled up into Tibet. By this time poor Heng Yo's relationship with the master had really begun to deteriorate, and he was back to wearing his permanently sad full-moon face. I wasn't doing that well myself. I was frustrated that we were doing all this running around, and I didn't know the full schedule. So I tried to ask the master what we were going to be doing in the coming weeks.

For the first time ever in my years of being his student, the master screamed directly at me. "When are we going to do this? When are we going to do that? What is this? What is that?" he yelled. "I'll tell you what this is! I'll tell you what that is! It's all just your scheming, calculating, climbing-on-conditions mind. That's what it is!" And with that he disappeared into his room and slammed the door.

Next stop, it turned out, was Sri Lanka, where we stayed with a wealthy layman who explained to us that he didn't have time to sit around and cultivate because he was too busy earning a living. The meals we'd been getting during our travels had been pretty marginal up to this point, but his staff served us up a delicious lunch of cheese sandwiches and vegetable soup.

"There's onions in this soup," said the master. "We can't eat it." He was right that monks don't eat the five pungent plants: onions, leeks, and the three others that I had forgotten the names of. But I was starved, and the soup smelled out-of-this-world delicious.

"I don't think there are onions in it," I contributed. Heng Yo and the master both pushed their soups aside, but I lifted mine up and drank it all down. Then I picked up theirs, one by one, and poured them down the hatch as well.

Next stop was Malaysia, Vietnam, and Taiwan: the pace was really starting to pick up, and people were waiting for us by the thousands everywhere we went. We were chauffeured around and looked after just like rock stars; we lectured to full houses, and after it was all over we'd be so high and wired that it was impossible to sleep. The master was besieged by hordes of laypeople who implored him to help solve their problems, and he did, answering all their questions deep into the night. His energy supply was nothing short of remarkable.

Later on we visited some of the main temples in Taiwan. The master, Heng Yo, and I had lunch with the old abbot of one monastery at his private table in front of a large assembly of monks and laypeople. When lunch was served, everyone at the table got normal, Chinese Buddhist vegetarian food. In the middle of the meal, however, the server came out and placed a hot loaf of freshly baked bread in front of the old abbot. Now I hadn't eaten any bread in a long time, and I had my eye on that loaf. What seemed like a long period of time passed, but no one passed the bread—no one touched it. So, while Shifu and the abbot talked, not wanting to interrupt them, I stood up, gathered in my robes, reached way across the table, and picked up the loaf of bread. I had just sat down with it when the master turned to me and said, "What are you doing? Put that back!" I was caught red-handed; his remarks stung me like a bee. I decided that if I couldn't have a piece of bread, then I wouldn't eat at all. I would simply go on a fast. So I went without food that day, and while everyone else ate, I sat there and pouted. I didn't think much of it at the time, but later, I would pay for it.

After Taiwan, we flew back to Hong Kong for a couple of days. The master had a few temples scattered around the archipelago. Without one word of warning or formal instruction, he told Heng Yo that he was sending him to be the abbot of one of them, Ci Hing Zi, which sat on a remote mountain on Lantau Island. Just like that, Yo left the whirlwind tour and was packed off to be the abbot of his own tiny temple in the middle of nowhere. I knew better than to ask the master about it, though. We flew alone together to Japan as winter began to settle into the Orient. This was our last stop before returning to America.

After returning from our hectic trip to Asia I attempted to settle into a more normal life at Gold Mountain. It wasn't going to happen. At his first formal lecture, the master told the entire community how much trouble Yo and I were to him while traveling. He said that we had caused the color of his hair to change from black to gray. To illustrate how we did this, he related the story about how I had reached for the abbot's loaf of bread at a temple in Taipei. It was funny the way he imitated me, standing up from his high seat and leaning way over to reach the imaginary loaf. But in my mind I knew that the honeymoon phase was behind me and I was now being tested. The days of fame and glory from my three-steps, one-bow pilgrimage were over.

Perhaps I should have known it was going to be this way. I had already seen the master pull the rug out from under a number of people, such as Kent. It was a definite pattern, almost predictable. People came in, got hooked on the Dharma, and in the honeymoon stage, Shifu praised and encouraged them so they would make initial progress on the path and perhaps become a monastic. They would gather knowledge, ability, power, and position, maybe even some fame. Then, inevitably, the big test would come barreling down the pike, their ego balloon would get popped, the iron gate would get slammed in their face, and the party would be over. Very few cultivators, it seemed, survived this critical stage of cultivation.

As things turned out, I wouldn't, either.

About this time, sexual desire began to become a real problem for me. I'd been completely celibate for several years, keeping all that vital energy inside, recirculating, spinning round and round and going nowhere. One night I was taking a shower in the men's lavatory area, a large room on the third floor that had four toilets and two shower stalls. I was indulging in the warm water, thinking of that last woman I had been with on the way home from the airport so many years ago. As I soaped down I could feel deepening lust slowly start to permeate my body. My temperature rose; my knees grew weak. My whole body and mind became filled with desire. Then, at that very instant, way off in the distance I thought I heard the master cough. I quickly got out of the shower, toweled off, and walked out of the bathroom, heading down the hall toward my room. The master's door slammed, and there he was walking toward me in the hallway. As we passed he looked right into my eyes and yelled, "Stupid!" There was no doubt about what he meant.

As luck would have it, a stunningly beautiful Asian woman appeared during a meditation session at one of the Dharma Realm Buddhist Association's branch monasteries in California not long after. All day long we were either sitting or walking around in a big circle, everyone dressed in traditional monastic garb. But she entered the line wearing a mini-skirt, displaying legs of copper-colored satin. You should have seen the trail of monks behind her attempting to walk straight. I myself swerved to the left and right like a ship without a rudder, trying to catch my bearings.

That evening, after the final sit, all was dark except for a big enchanting moon hung up in the sky, rendering everything mysterious and wonderful. I went out walking, and I passed Shifu in the inner courtyard with this alluring new person. He said to me, "Kuo Yu, why don't you escort this young woman to her quarters?"

My mouth dropped open. What kind of a cosmic joke was this? Should I walk the lovely lady through the darkness to her room, putting my vows to the test? Or should I say no and disobey the request of my teacher? My brain felt like a scrambled egg. I had no idea what to do, so I just stood there like an idiot. Shifu solved the problem by answering his own question.

"Maybe I better see her up there," he announced. And they were off into the night.

I knew I was being tested, but I just couldn't come around. Shifu completely withdrew his favor, ignoring me entirely, and afflictions by the hundreds began to manifest in my life. I slacked off in my cultivation, and my mind became filled with limitless desires. I started to skip ceremonies here and there, even though I knew that the master wanted us, at the very least, to attend morning and evening services.

Bit by bit, doubt crept in. Things that shouldn't bother me bothered me to no end. The DRBA had just bought five hundred acres of land in northern California's Ukiah Valley, the former grounds of the county's nineteenth-century insane asylum. They were planning to convert the compound into what would eventually become the City of Ten Thousand Buddhas, one of the largest Buddhist communities in the Western Hemisphere. *Why*, I grumbled when I saw the building plans for it, *did the abbot want to make the compound's gymnasium into a buddha hall? It was a perfect full-court basketball area! We should leave it that way. Then we could put together a team of Buddhists and take on the locals. It would be a great way for them to get to know us. And why were we still doing all these Chinese ceremonies? This is America. We should be doing American things. We should be more like the San Francisco Zen Center! They have a grocery store, a beach resort, a neighborhood park, an organic farm, a veggie restaurant. Why did everything here have to be so Chinese?*

I let thoughts like these ramble through my brain, and they took on a life of their own. My afflictions turned into resentments. After a while it seemed like I was hanging on to monkhood by a thread.

I thought that maybe I needed a break from everyone in the American sangha, including Shifu, so when Heng Yo came back from serving at Ci Hing Zi, I volunteered to take his place. But things were even worse there. While the monastery's two elderly bhikshunis worked all day in the gardens or performed upkeep on the network of trails around the mountain where the monastery was located (actually, the place was carved into the side of it), I mostly sat around in a daze, trying to figure out what to do with myself. Every once in a while I'd go to Hong Kong on "business"—ostensibly to send mail, buy books, or whatever. In reality, I couldn't stand sitting around any longer and had to get out and do something. The old bhikshunis got really upset and worried when I left the mountain, as well they should have—the sights and sounds of the city always managed to turn my head around. Sexual desire, of course, was the first to rear its dragon head, and although I never did anything, by day's end I would be sick with lust. To make matters worse, people would constantly stare at me and point. (I was 6'4" and the average Hong Kong person was between 5' and 5'2".) My whole life, I had never let what people thought upset me, but now that I was on the decline, their mocking and pointing was boring under my skin, getting to me in a way I wasn't proud of.

Once a month or so, I was invited into the monastery's main hall to perform a grand ceremony—I believe it was called "Feeding Those with Flaming Mouths." This was a very important ceremony for the cultivators at the hall, and it was an honor to be asked to facilitate it.

At the last one I attended, the faithful Cantonese lay ladies requested that I wear the bright red robes of an abbot. The ceremony was in Chinese, and I didn't have the slightest idea what it was all about or what I was supposed to do, but they indicated not to worry, just to follow along and stand in the middle, so I did. The bells and drums and gongs banged away and the incense filled the room as the ceremony gathered momentum. A kindly little lady—everyone in the room, about thirty people, was a lady—elbowed me when it was time for me to do something like bow or stand up, and I was doing pretty well at faking my way through the thing.

After about an hour of this she handed me a huge platter of peanuts and candy, smiled at me with a big toothy grin, and indicated that I should start throwing the items around the room. I gave her the universal look for "Are you shitting me?" She said no and threw the first handful. So obligingly, I took a handful and threw it across the room. Everyone smiled and nodded their approval. Hey! This was fun! I grabbed another handful and really gave it a toss. They smiled and nodded even more. Something inside of me broke. Out of nowhere I burst into laughter.

This was the most preposterous thing I had ever done in my life. Here I was in the middle of the Orient, dressed in ceremonial Tang dynasty robes, surrounded by these incredibly pure old Cantonese ladies, all about a foot and a half shorter than I, and I was nonchalantly tossing candy and peanuts around in the master's own buddha hall. Soon I was roaring with laughter. All the ladies joined in, I threw that candy all over the hall, and we partied! But that night I called the States and requested a transfer back. I didn't belong in Chinese culture. I needed to be in America.

I returned from Hong Kong, tired and lonely, in late 1977. By then the construction had been finished on the City of Ten Thousand Buddhas and the master had moved the HQ of DRBA operations from San Francisco to Ukiah, over one hundred miles north. The male monastics were housed in Tathagata Monastery, a 280-room building that used to be a cell block for the criminally insane. I tried to adjust to living there, but I felt a little insane myself. Just as had happened in Hong Kong, the new environment didn't help me get back on track; I might have been in my own country, but I was still living like the ancient Chinese, and the master was still ignoring me.

And yet, even as I came more and more undone, I secretly hoped that Shifu would give me just one more sign that he was watching over me, one more sign that he cared for me and that his awesome psychic powers were still intact. Just one more miracle—that's all I needed to turn everything around!

I got one—but not until it was too late.

At the monastery we had this old yellow school bus that someone had donated, on which one of our resident artists, Matthew Leeds, had painted an incredibly beautiful black dragon. It was just like the one I saw in the sky the day my bowing pilgrimage ended.

One day soon after my return from Hong Kong I took the bus down to the Bay Area to get a load of furniture and books to bring back up to the City of Ten Thousand Buddhas. I left Ukiah in the morning and had the bus loaded by mid-afternoon. On the way back up north, I was driving past Vallejo when I spotted one of my old submarine bars, the Horse and Cow, alongside the freeway. (In my defense, it was hard to miss—there was a giant submarine mounted on the roof.) The Horse and Cow had quite a history; it moved around the Bay Area depending on where the majority of submarine sailors hung out. I remember it downtown on Eddy Street, then out by the gate at Hunter's Point shipyard. Now it was in Vallejo, in order to be near the sub sailors attending nuclear power school. What a bar! It was filled with submarine paraphernalia wall-to-wall, everything from pictures and plaques to depth gauges and controls. I had seen some incredible things happen in the H&C, especially on those nights when the "seagulls," the girls that followed the boats, were around. It was an atmosphere where a guy could really be himself and cut loose.

As I was innocently driving by, the thought occurred to me, *Why not stop in just for old time's sake and see what's happening?* There wouldn't be any harm in it, I reasoned. I was wearing baggy cotton work clothes and I had a watch cap to pull over my bald head. Certainly no one would recognize me; I hadn't been in there in a decade.

I pulled the bus off the freeway and parked in the lot behind the bar. It was dark when I walked inside. Loopy, the owner, was tending bar. A few people were in the back playing pool, and the jukebox was on. My plan was simply to sit alone in a corner, order a soft drink, and quietly observe what was happening.

But when Loopy approached to take my order, something peculiar happened. Instead of asking for a 7Up, the words "bourbon and 7" spilled out of my mouth. It was a twisted thought—there was no explaining it then, and I still couldn't explain it to you now.

The drink was placed before me. I picked it up—the first alcohol to pass my lips in seven years—and poured it down the hatch. Then I drank another and another. After most of my inhibitions had dissolved, I joined the group in the back playing pool. I was having a great time, but even in my drunken, blissful stupor I could tell that one of the players was a psycho. He was a great big guy they called Patrick, who just stood there and laughed insanely at everything I did.

Before I knew it, it was closing time and they were asking everybody to leave. I was the last out the door, not the least bit anxious to stop my binge. In the front lot an American sedan filled with all the pool players was getting ready to leave. I asked them where they were going.

"We're going partying!" someone exclaimed.

"Is it OK if I come along?" I asked.

"Sure, hop in."

There was no seating available in the car, so I hurled myself into the back over the top of everyone else, and we were off to the party. I'd forgotten all about the dragon bus, not to mention my vows as a monk.

The party was in a poorly lit house somewhere across town in Vallejo. I joined the group in a large circle in the living room, where they were passing around joints and drinks. I took off my work boots to relax my feet; no one seemed to notice me in the chaos of the party. I latched onto a drink and tried to scope out what was going on. As I listened to the conversation, though, I could hardly believe my drunken ears. These people were hoods, and they were all getting ready to hold up a liquor store.

"Jack, you cover the back and make sure no one comes around."

"Ed, you stay in the car and be ready to haul ass when we come out of there."

"Carol, I want you to go in with me and distract him while I case the joint."

Suddenly I came to my senses a little bit. I needed to get out—quick. I stood up and walked into the bathroom to take a leak first. Right in the middle of it, I heard crazy-sounding laughter, and turned around to see none else but Patrick filling up the doorway. He had a shit-eating grin on his face and he looked totally crazed. I was still holding my unit. Patrick, on the other hand, was holding a pocket knife.

He didn't waste any time. Grabbing me by my gray arhat jacket, he jabbed the knife through it, cutting it top to bottom.

"Patrick, maybe we can talk about this!" I yelled.

Patrick didn't answer. Instead, he pulled at the other side of the jacket and cut that part open top to bottom too, missing my flesh by a fraction of an inch as he laughed like the madman he was. I didn't like this game, but there was nothing I could do. After the third pass through my jacket, though, I mustered all the adrenaline I could, burst from his grip, and lunged for the door. He swung at me as I passed and hit me firmly on the head, knocking off my watch cap in the process.

Adrenaline rushing, I ran through the house and out through the screen door, no doubt leaving the outline of one scared human being in the frayed wire. I was at flank speed when I left the porch, and suddenly there was nothing under me as I tumbled through empty space, finally landing on the sloping lawn below. I was without shoes or hat as I ran frantically through the streets of Vallejo, trying to find my way back to the Horse and Cow. Eventually I found it, jumped in the bus, and drove hurriedly north and out of town.

The next morning I awoke on the floor of the bus, hung over to beat the band. I stood up and looked around. I recognized the bus, but I had no idea where I was. I was parked in the middle of a vast field somewhere in the Napa Valley. The bus was covered with mud inside and out. Then I saw my jacket, all sliced to threads. Abruptly, I remembered everything.

The unmitigated terror I felt at that moment cannot be expressed in words. In one fell swoop I had broken my sacred vows and gone back to being a drunken sailor. I'd almost been killed. And where were my boots and my hat?

I cranked up the bus, drove out of the field, and managed to find my way back to the City of Ten Thousand Buddhas. I drove in the back way, parked the bus, slipped into the monastery, and got cleaned up before anybody saw me. No one had the slightest suspicion I had gone astray.

No one, that is, except the master. I knew that he knew; of that there was no doubt.

At that time at the City of Ten Thousand Buddhas, they were just preparing to start up a seven-day Chan session in the buddha hall. I was overwhelmed with guilt and fear, and I had no idea what to do. Eventually I decided that there was nothing *to* do but go to the session and meditate like everything was normal. Maybe after the seven days I would know.

On opening night, which was always a big occasion with the sangha and laity, about one hundred people were in attendance. At around seven in the evening we gathered and commenced the rapid walking in a giant circle around the perimeter of the hall. We walked in descending order: the monks in front, then the nuns, then the laymen, followed by the lay-women. Because I had been around longer than any of the monks there, I was first in line. First! Imagine how I felt, carrying this giant sin around inside my soul, while outwardly trying to manifest the appearance of a holy guy. I'll tell you how I felt—I felt like shit.

We walked briskly for half an hour or so as more people straggled in. Finally the master arrived, carrying with him his ceremonial wooden sword used for "striking up the qi." We walked with him for another five minutes, the master last, me first. Then in the traditional manner, the master banged his sword on the floor and everyone immediately froze in their tracks. He slowly started working his way around the room, starting at the end of the line. He stopped in front of each participant, looked them squarely in the eyes, and gave them a light ceremonial strike on the shoulders signifying that they should strike up their energies and strike out all their false thinking. He was on his way to me, and my brain went into maximum overload. I was scared to death. The master didn't say much as he walked around the room, maybe a special word or two to someone who needed it. But when he got to me, he stopped and stared at me with a distant smile as if giving my brain a thorough reading. In fact, that's exactly what he was doing, and when he got through looking at the Horse and Cow event, he focused on me and said dryly, "Well, well. It looks like the sailor lost his hat again."

That was it. Nothing more. In those few words he summed up the entirety of my first three decades on the planet. He showed me in that one sentence that he knew everything, that he still cared about me—and that he was helpless to save me from my own karma. I would have to work things out for myself. My mind exploded in a riot of emotions. Some of the people chuckled politely, not knowing what was going on. And then the Chan began.

Not for me, though. I was finished, and I knew it. All the wiring inside was short-circuited. I could no longer function. I had broken the rules, and I didn't know what to do except leave—and so I did. The next day, I disrobed and fled the monastery.

12. AFTER THE MONASTERY

No one could have been more confused than I when I ran out the gate of the City of Ten Thousand Buddhas. The demons of my latent alcoholism, which would guide me right back into the binge-drinking patterns from my sailor days, lay waiting to bring me to hell. I didn't know I was an alcoholic at the time; all I knew was that I wanted to obliterate my unbearable anguish, so I reached out for what was most familiar to me: booze. I drank to kill the pain, and the alcohol created even more pain and remorse.

Driving an old Toyota I'd bought from a faithful layman, I was nailed with a drunk driving ticket before even getting out of California. Once back in the Northwest, it was not long before I'd lost everything of value. My career as a monk vanished, my Dharma friends were gone, and I was alone in the world. Alcohol muddled my brain, and in the darkness, seeds of desire sprouted like weeds. I frequented bars, chased women, started smoking again, and drank to forget it all.

I found work as an assistant engineer on a wreck of a freezer ship, the motor vessel *Polar Bear*, for a long summer of salmon tendering. No one knew that I was an ex-monk in hiding. The owner, seeing that I didn't have enough to do while the ship was at anchor, yanked me out of the engine room and put me to work on the assembly line. Ankle-deep in fish roe and salmon guts, I had plenty of time to contemplate the nature of my fall.

After the first two months, I couldn't stand it any longer. I borrowed a motorboat and went upriver until I found the only bar in the area, the Red

Dog Saloon, where I promptly went in and got curb-crawling, shit-faced, snot-flying drunk. The next morning I found myself out in the scrub, flat on my back, staring up at a cloudy, menacing sky. After a while, it all came back to me: a couple of fishermen had bushwhacked me outside the bar and beaten me to a bloody pulp.

After the ship returned to Seattle, my downhill slide continued. There were many more pathetic incidents.

Carrying a burden of unbearable guilt and shame, I kept trying to straighten out but seemed powerless to do so. What I needed more than anything was to talk to someone about my problems. On one occasion I wrote a letter to the master asking for his advice on how to stop drinking. "Why don't you sew your lips shut and try pouring the booze through your nose!" came his written reply.

When no sympathy from the master came, I tried to settle down in Seattle. I even married and became a father, but I wasn't ready for any of it. I found a job in a local diesel/generator shop, and every night after work I'd go out for drinks with the boys. One morning my wife asked me where I'd left the car.

"Outside, where I always park it," I replied.

"I suggest you look out the window," she said. I looked, but the car was not there. I hopped on a bus and spent the rest of the day riding up and down the streets of Seattle until I finally found the car. A bum was sleeping in the front seat, and the back was filled with over one hundred loaves of bread.

When I returned to the house, my wife, who used to work in a detox facility, looked me in the eyes and uttered the sentence that I will never forget: "Tim, you are an alcoholic!" Her truth hurt, yet I knew she was right the instant she spoke. But since alcoholism is a disease characterized by denial, I had to keep drinking just to make sure she was right.

Eventually, inevitably, my wife and I separated, and there was no one left to interfere with my drinking. I got a job on a National Oceanic and Atmospheric Administration ship, and with a loan from Veterans Affairs bought a house in the suburbs of Seattle. I didn't have enough self-esteem to live in it, however, so I took in a Cambodian refugee family while I camped in a seventeen-foot trailer in the backyard. It was there that I drank myself down to the murky bottom.

One morning, waking up to face all the usual horrors of what had become three-day hangovers, I experienced an unusual awakening. Why was I doing this? Why was I drinking myself into oblivion when there was absolutely no reason for it? I had a good job, a wonderful child, a cute house, and no wife to blame. I was free to do whatever I wanted. The drinking just didn't make sense. At that moment I was able to find genuine resolve. From the bottom of my heart I said to myself, "I don't care what it takes—I'm going to quit drinking, get sober, and stay sober!" I called the captain of my ship and asked him if he could arrange to send me to an inpatient alcoholism treatment center. He obliged.

I consider the day I got sober as a true awakening and a major turning point in my life. While I was at the monastery, I had followed the rules because I had to, but I couldn't be sure if I was really doing it or just going along with external pressure. Now I would have a chance, completely on my own, to start over and internalize the rules, to take personal responsibility for my sobriety and spiritual recovery. That small but solid thought, mustered up from the depths of my miserable, drunken soul, was the beginning of a new life.

After accumulating a reasonable amount of sobriety, a year or so, I decided it was time to return to the monastery and make amends. I took the thousand-mile trip to Ukiah, California, to the City of Ten Thousand Buddhas, and to the master.

Prior to the evening Dharma talk I lit incense, circumambulated the Buddha and bowed three times, kneeled, and made my formal repentance. The master observed from the high seat; about a hundred disciples were also in attendance. Following my repentance, the master said, "Kuo Yu, like most people, you are a mixture of good and bad. Fortunately, you have more good than bad. Just work on making the good points more, the bad points less. Everyone makes mistakes, so don't worry; everything is OK. Patience is the thing you need to work on now—extreme patience. I know you want to leave the home life again, but you have karma to work out. Stay there for now. Don't doubt Buddhism, and don't go to spoil. You have been a very positive influence for Buddhism in the West. You are welcome to come here and cultivate anytime."

Never, ever, have I felt the weight of such a burden lifted from my shoulders. I was forgiven. I was a free man. I felt like I could fly!

That was then; this is now.

The master, I'm sorry to say, is dead and gone. His final words: "I came from empty space, and to empty space I return." Before he passed away, I felt the need to see him one more time, so I made the arrangements, drove to California, and finagled my way in. He was on his deathbed.

I guess I was vaguely hoping that he would transmit the Dharma to me or something—he had told Heng Yo and me once on the Asia tour that he was going to, although he never did. But no, I told myself, that didn't matter. I just wanted to thank him for all he'd done for me and ask his forgiveness for being such a pain in the butt.

I also had a question about pure eating. Following my teenage daughter Jetti's example, I had gone back to my strict vegetarian diet. I'd been doing fine with it for over a year, but I had a big question that was eating away at me. I was living in a waterfront cabin on a saltwater bay, and the shoreline was filled with succulent, world-class oysters. It was great to shuck them right on the beach, leaving the shells there, then soak the little buggers overnight in olive oil and herbs and broil them the next day to golden brown on both sides. What a delicacy! So my question was: Since oysters have no arms or legs, no eyes or face, and they grow on rocks, then they must not be an animal. Weren't they more or less a vegetable? And if so, what harm would it be if I ate them, especially since they conveniently spawned right in my own front yard?

This was the big life-and-death question on my mind, one I had discussed with no one.

When I entered the master's room, his attendant announced, "Kuo Yu is here."

The master responded, "Kuo Yu, don't become a fish!"

There is a stage of spiritual development along the bodhisattva path that is called *avaivartika*, Sanskrit for "irreversible." At this stage, one's thoughts, position, and practice no longer turn back toward confusion. I remember when I was the cook at the monastery and I had just taken up the practice of eating only one meal a day. I was doing really well for several days, but one morning I couldn't stand it any longer and decided to have some breakfast. I remember it clearly: I was heading for the icebox. In fact, I had my hand on the icebox door when I looked out in the hallway to see the master walking by. He was smiling as he walked down the hall. Then suddenly he stopped and began walking backward, retracing his steps back down the hall, around the corner, and out of sight. Not a word was spoken, but I got the message.

Well, once again I hadn't even asked my question, and I received a response. It was also a pun on my name, because *yu* means "to constantly go beyond" (or overdo things), and another character, *yu*, means "fish." If I ate oysters, therefore, I might be reborn as a sea creature, a realm where only one in ten thousand doesn't die a violent death.

Then the master kidded me about a letter I'd written a while back, suggesting that there were too many ceremonies at the City of Ten Thousand Buddhas.

"There are many, many Dharma doors," he said. "Not just one. It's good for people to study many doors."

"OK, Shifu. I agree."

"How old is your daughter?" Shifu asked.

"She's fourteen, Shifu. She's going to a private boarding school, and, well, she's doing just great," I rambled on.

"I know," replied the master. "Who is going to take care of you when you're old?" he asked.

"I don't know, Shifu." I could feel tears welling up. "All I know is that I just want to cultivate the Way, Shifu."

"Did you read the latest *Vajra Bodhi Sea?*" the master asked, referring to the monthly magazine of the Dharma Realm Buddhist Association. "The story about the camphor tree?"

"No, Shifu."

"Get him a copy of the article," he instructed his attendant. When the attendant brought me the magazine, I sat and read about a camphor tree on Potala Mountain in China that had taken refuge with the master. The story ended with these words of exhortation: "Whoever you are, if you have a true and sincere mind, if you are not careless in the least, if you do not go along with what worldly people do, but do the contrary, then you will be able to attain the benefit of Buddhism. Whether you are a left-home or layperson, you should be true Buddhists. Don't be like ordinary people: greedy, fighting, seeking, selfish, and self-benefiting, not letting a moment go by from morning to night without acting falsely. This is most important! These six great principles are the first step toward learning Buddhism and eventually accomplishing buddhahood. Don't forget them! Don't neglect them! We should learn to take more losses and not take any advantages."

I bowed to the master.

He smiled and said, "OK, time for a rest."

EPILOGUE:
TIPS AND TRICKS ALONG THE PATH

1. Produce the Bodhi Mind: Resolve

The resolve to awaken, or *bodhichitta*, is the catalyst for spiritual transformation. There won't be any progress down the path unless you've first made up your mind to walk it. But once you do, you will already be reckoning with enlightenment, initiating a fundamental change within the depths of your heart that will produce miraculous results. The benefits of Buddhism are in direct proportion to the energy put into practice.

In Buddhism they say that if you wish to understand the nature of the universe, contemplate that all things, inside and out, are made from mind alone. Nirvana and samsara, heaven and hell, all take place in the here and now. Thus your attitude is your kingdom—one you take with you everywhere.

It pays, then, to have an attitude of gratitude. That doesn't mean you go around being grateful for every little thing. (Who would you be grateful to, anyway?) It means that you really start to appreciate the wonders of the universe around you. You look at it through fresh eyes, seeing beyond your old personal interests and concepts right on through to the miracle of life unfolding in every moment: the sun shining on your face, the sound of a bird, a couple arguing, the roar of a passing diesel, the smell of fragrant incense, the joy and innocence of youth. This new attitude of having an alert, alive, open mind is a natural carryover from sitting meditation and will positively affect the rest of your waking moments.

2. *Finding a Teacher: A True Friend; a Good, Knowing Advisor; a Buddha*

It's best if you can find a genuine teacher, but unfortunately they are rare indeed. Beware—there are countless false teachers in the world. Many use the language of Buddhism to give credence to themselves. These masters of deception are bound for hell and will gladly take you along for the trip. Without a proper teacher, a cultivator can easily slide off the path. When the Way grows an inch, the demons grow a foot. Be careful!

A true teacher is one of infinite merit and virtue, vast knowledge and wisdom, awesome deportment, far-reaching vows, pure precepts, myriad practices, inconceivable spiritual penetrations, and certified accomplishment. He or she is like a dam full of water, to whom we come with our empty cups. In one hundred different ways he or she instills the spirit and the will to cultivate so you are inspired to do what you have to do. A true teacher can easily point out attachments and may even use the group to give you feedback on your state. He or she easily disrupts routines, habits, positions, and goal-oriented behavior. A true teacher teaches the bitter practices that bring about a sweet mind. Using praise, scolding, threats, encouragement, whatever, he or she may be able to maneuver us into position where we are like rats up against a wall, so we can quickly open enlightenment. In these and so many other ways, a true teacher shows us how to forge a vajra, indestructible mind. If you don't run off when things get difficult, you can learn a thing or two.

Master Hua was the only such teacher I know of—a hard act to follow. In the absence of a good teacher, however, one can only fall back upon the advice of the Buddha, who counseled that when he entered nirvana his disciples should take refuge in the precepts. If you take them, the five lay precepts will become the everlasting foundation of your practice. They are (1) not to kill, (2) not to steal, (3) not to engage in sexual misconduct, (4) not to lie, and (5) not to consume intoxicants.

3. Study: A Chart and Compass

The written Dharma can be found in the Buddhist canon: the sutras, the *shastras*, and the monastic code, or *vinaya*. Many Buddhist sutras are in print in English and can be found in good bookstores. Buy these if you like. Some of them are pretty good.

Collect these books and work through one or two of them at all times. I take a stack to sea with me. I have the *Brahma Net Sutra* on my nightstand, the *Avatamsaka Prologue* on my desk, and the *Shurangama Sutra* at my reading chair. Everywhere I go there's something good to read. (I also have the latest issue of *PC Magazine* for the john, but that's neither here nor there.)

Treat the sutras with respect; they are sacred texts. Reading them will increase your wisdom, samadhi, and faith.

4. Praxis: Walking the Path, Cultivating the Way, Action

Build a personal practice.

Your life is your practice; there's no getting away from it. So make every minute count. There are eighty-four thousand Dharma doors to pick from. Study many, but choose to practice what most pleases and interests you. If you visit Gold Mountain for a while, don't come home with rocks and dirt. Go for the gold. Don't waste your time with all the trappings and crap in the attic. Create your own rituals. Thus, I prefer to work mostly with Chan meditation. Sitting, walking, lying, standing, I try to never be apart from it, and plan on practicing it the best I can until the day I die.

Start with your body.

Within your body is a Buddhist monastery. Take good care of it with proper diet. As a practicing vegetarian, especially if you go vegan and don't eat dairy products, you'll need to take a B12 supplement, and look for plenty of zinc, iron, calcium, and vitamin D in your vegetables. Organic vegetables are the best.

Regular exercise is necessary to help you accomplish the Way. Take the time to learn a set of hatha yoga or tai chi so you can stretch your muscles and build up strength. Besides relieving your aches and pains and making you feel great and full of energy, exercise will relieve tension and stress and help calm and center you. It will strengthen your qi, open you up, and prepare the body for sitting meditation. In the morning you get the energy moving; in the evening you calm it down. I can't say enough about the benefits of regular exercise.

And if you suffer from alcoholism, depression, or other serious physical, mental, or emotional problems, please get the help you need from professionals. Buddhism isn't a cure-all for every human ailment.

Practice sitting meditation every day. It is said that sitting in full lotus trying to still one's mind has more merit and virtue than filling the ten directions with offerings of temples and shrines. The goal is to be able to sit in full lotus for one hour at a time—that's one standard-issue Gold Mountain sit. Of course, most people won't be able to sit in full lotus right away, but make it your goal and make progress a little bit at a time.

Create a cozy sitting area in your home. You'll need a blanket or rug for a floor mat, and then a zafu or sitting pillow of some type to elevate your rear end. Try to start out your sit in full lotus, if only for a few minutes at first. You can always downshift to half lotus when it gets too uncomfortable. In any case, try to get a three-point foundation touching the floor: two knees and your butt. If you need to, place a shoe, rag, or bolster under a knee to let it touch down.

The next step is to gently tighten up and lift your butt muscles. Now that you are grounded, straighten out and lengthen your spine. Imagine that you are trying to use willpower to lift yourself right off the floor. Or imagine that there is a string lifting you up, erect and alert. During the sitting period, constantly re-evaluate your posture and make sure that you haven't started to slouch. This can be very subtle, but once you start to slouch in the slightest, then your mind and your meditation go with it. Be alert! Sit bolt upright! Be totally aware! Let your body and mind become a conduit through which you witness the universal energies flowing endlessly.

I suggest keeping a journal to keep track of your time in meditation, exercise, and other practice-oriented activities. This might sound trivial, but I've tried with and without keeping track, and keeping track makes a big difference. You'll be surprised how this reinforces and rewards your practice, especially if you're doing it on your own.

On a typical busy workday, my own log might read:

40 minutes lotus

20 minutes yoga

1 hour study (including the name of text)

3-mile walk (with the name of person or golden retriever)

30 minutes lotus

But don't stop here. The bodhisattva path involves the six major actions of the paramitas, or perfections. Of course, you can't keep track of these in a journal, but they should become as natural to you as breathing:

(1) **Giving:** Participate in something bigger than yourself, something that will be around when you've gone and that you'll feel satisfied to watch grow. Sweep, haul garbage, clean toilets, attend lectures. Things will clear up fast. Open yourself to subtle changes.

Give up fear. Surrender to your life, your marriage, your spouse, your program, to now, to responsibilities, and stop trying to escape. Give up running and start surrendering to life.

If you like giving, you can give your nature, body, and mind to the world. Giving is karma that creates blessings and honor, but to cut off desire and stop false thinking is the true field of blessings.

(2) Morality: The five precepts, listed above, provide a basic set of guidelines to protect you from passing into a state of emptiness where you deny cause and effect. Following them also destroys vast amounts of offensive karma. If you can learn to enjoy following the rules, the discipline will give you energy and a sense of cultivation.

True morality is when the eyes, ears, nose, tongue, body, and brain are not defiled by the six sense objects.

(3) Patience: Acquire patience for the long haul: it's a lifetime commitment. Accord with living beings. Like everybody, whether they like you or not—they are all future buddhas. Let others be number one, and don't be afraid to take a loss now and then. Be patient with anything made of earth, air, wind, or fire. Be patient with all people and all dharmas.

(4) Vigor: Get up earlier, but limit your fields of activity to the ones that are most important. Cut off outflows as best possible. Enjoy life! Emit sparks! Fly! Then turn your newfound energy back into cultivation and the community of enlightenment.

(5) Samadhi: Remain unmoved, always. Demons will come and test you. Be fearless; guard your light.

(6) Way (Wisdom): Appear dumb, be wise.

Music comes from lessons and practice. Same with the Dharma. Study and practice of the Dharma leads to awakenings, both gradual and sudden. But don't worry about enlightenment; just go through the process. Plant seeds, and the results will come of themselves.

Zen is not just sitting quietly. It's a dynamic way of life. Keep cool, hang on, don't lose your humor. It's just when things are all fouled up that you test your mettle.

5. *Identify with the Buddha*

From the above-mentioned resolve, study, and practice you can gradually, or even suddenly, start identifying with the Buddha. This starts with understanding the Buddhist teaching of no-self.

The self is nothing more than a conditioned construct that we are taught to believe in from birth onward. Our language drives it home. "I want this, I feel that, I did that." Subject, verb, object. Buddhism says that these views are false and illusory. The self is a convenience for getting by in the conditioned world, but we shouldn't take a thief for our own son.

It's like a Chevrolet. There really is no Chevrolet; it's just a collection of parts. A bunch of steel, vinyl, rubber, wires, fabric. The self is no different. It's simply a temporary coming together of form, feeling, perceptions, karma, and consciousness. In our meditations we come to realize that there is no "me" to find inside.

The sutras are filled with explanations of the Dharma of no-self. In the *Heart Sutra*, for example, it says that in emptiness there is no form, feeling, perception, karma, or consciousness. No eye, ear, nose, tongue, body, mind. Anything at all that can be identified as self is wiped out. It leaves you with nothing to hang on to except your infinite and intrinsic buddha nature.

That's why Buddhism encourages us to make our shift of identity now. If we continue to identify with the five *skandhas*—the "heaps" of form, sensations, perceptions, mental activity, and consciousness that comprise our mental and physical existence—then at the time of old age, sickness, and death, there will be a lot of suffering. If we identify with our buddha nature, then we can gladly let go of those heaps.

If you're like me, however, you'll probably want to try on some new identities along the way. For decades, I've wanted to be a great monk, a great teacher, a patriarch, and so on. It's only when we let go of all that that we can become more infinite.

PHOTO CREDITS AND CAPTIONS

cover. Tim prostrating.

page ii. Tim on pilgrimage.

page 5. Jetti and Tim, 1987.

page 21. Complete Testu family.

Back row: Joseph (Father), Tim, Terry, Kathleen, Virginia (Mom).

Front row: Mary Jo, Kirk, Mark John, Matthew.

page 91. Gold Mountain monastery, San Francisco.

page 108. The author receiving ordination. Courtesy of the Dharma Realm Buddhist Association.

page 134. Shifu and Tim with pie.

page 140. Heng Yo and Tim on the road.

page 162. Heng Yo and Tim on a rainy day during the bowing pilgrimage.

page 169. Heng Yo, Shifu, and Tim on the roof of the Gold Mountain Monastery, San Francisco.

page 194. Tim wearing a tarp as a robe.

page 196. The photo of Jeanette is by Lisa Pedersen. The photo of Emma is by Seth Miranda.

ABOUT THE CONTRIBUTORS

TIM TESTU was born in 1944 to an Irish Catholic family in West Seattle. He had the typically free-range childhood of that era complete with pulling pranks on nuns, roaming the streets till dark, and making his six younger siblings cry. After being thrown out of his Catholic high school, he signed up for the navy and squeaked through six years with an honorable discharge, doing well for himself so long as he stayed away from alcohol. After the navy, Tim found his spiritual home in the presence of Hsuan Hua: the genuine article, an enlightened teacher. He spent the next ten years in diligent study of Chan Buddhism with only a few slips with candy bars and cigarettes. But eventually his disease tracked him down despite the seclusion of the monastery, and in 1983, he sought treatment for alcoholism. From that time on, he practiced a different Middle Way, trying to balance his Buddhist precepts with the demands of the world: bills to pay, a child to raise, a career to handle, a cancer diagnosis to manage, ex-wives to get along with, and of course, his alcoholism to face.

Tim never did anything halfway, including both drinking and striving for liberation. He died of leukemia in 1998 after packing ten lifetimes into fifty-two years.

JEANETTE TESTU, Tim's daughter, grew up and continues to live in beautiful western Washington. She works as a disability law paralegal and is now studying to be a pastry chef—not due to legal burnout but for the puzzle of perfecting a recipe and the joy of feeding her loves. She has had the privilege of helping families of children with special needs for over ten years. She has a fabulous teenage son, Liam, who plays lots of instruments and kindly eats green macarons and cookies with coriander. On any given day she follows three to five of the precepts. She values her unconventional upbringing and applies many Buddhist principles to her messy modern life.

EMMA VARVALOUCAS is the executive editor of *Tricycle: The Buddhist Review*, where she has worked with writers from across the Buddhist traditions for almost a decade. After a childhood spent as a bunhead in tights and pointe shoes, she now moonlights as a professional aerialist and aerial dance teacher. A student in the Tibetan Karma Kagyu and Nyingma lineages, she strives to be less of a terrible practitioner every day. This is her first book-length project.

WHAT TO READ NEXT FROM WISDOM PUBLICATIONS

Saltwater Buddha

A Surfer's Quest to Find Zen on the Sea

Jaimal Yogis

"Heartfelt, honest, and deceptively simple. It's great stuff with the words 'Cult Classic' stamped all over it."—Alex Wade, author of *Surf Nation*

Unsubscribe

Opt Out of Delusion, Tune In to Truth

Josh Korda

Foreword by Noah Levine

"Josh Korda makes Buddhism relatable and fresh, weaves in neuroscience and psychology, and serves it all up with a heaping dollop of candor, fearlessness, and wit. This book is a how-to guide for people wanting to learn how to face demons, forge deeper connections, sit comfortably in their skin, and step away from the distractions of social media and mindlessness of consumerism—things we all know will never leave us satisfied. Tune in and unsubscribe."—Cara Buckley of the *New York Times*

I Wanna Be Well
How a Punk Found Peace and You Can Too
Miguel Chen and Rod Meade Sperry

A punk rocker's guide to finding peace with yourself and the world—even through life's most painful moments.

Hardcore Zen
Punk Rock, Monster Movies, and the Truth About Reality
Brad Warner

"*Hardcore Zen* is to Buddhism what the Ramones were to rock and roll: a clear-cut, no-bulls**t offering of truth."—Miguel Chen, Teenage Bottlerocket

Chan Heart, Chan Mind
A Meditation on Serenity and Growth
Master Guojun
Edited by Kenneth Wapner

"Simple, lovely writing, vivid detail, and understanding of the Chan path give this short book a gentle spirit."—*Publishers Weekly*

Mindfulness in Plain English
Bhante Gunaratana

"A classic—one of the very best English sources for authoritative explanations of mindfulness."—Daniel Goleman, author of *Emotional Intelligence*

About Wisdom Publications

Wisdom Publications is the leading publisher of classic and contemporary Buddhist books and practical works on mindfulness. To learn more about us or to explore our other books, please visit our website at wisdompubs.org or contact us at the address below.

Wisdom Publications
199 Elm Street
Somerville, Massachusetts 02144
USA

We are a 501(c)(3) organization, and donations in support of our mission are tax deductible.

Wisdom Publications is affiliated with the Foundation for the Preservation of the Mahayana Tradition (FPMT).